C000110066

TJ Publishers

Advantage Business Centre

132-134 Great Ancoats Street

Manchester

M4 6DE

Tel: 0141 880 6839

Fax: 0870 124 9189

e-mail: teejaypublishers@btinternet.com

web page: www.teejaypublishers.co.uk

© TeeJay Publishers 2014
   First Edition published by TeeJay Publishers - March 2014

All rights in this book are reserved. No part of this book may be copied
or reproduced in any format, including electronic, without the express
permission of the authors in accordance with the Copyright, Design
and Patents Act of 1988.

Any person or organisation who makes unauthorised copies of any part
of this book may be liable to prosecution and possible civil claims for
damages.

Printed by :-

Elanders Ltd
Merlin Way
New York Business Park
North Tyneside NE27 0QG
Registered in England number 3788582
http://www.elanders.com/uk

Year 3 Textbook

Book 3

Produced by members of the TeeJay Writing Group

T Strang, J Geddes and J Cairns.

Front and Back Cover designed by *Fraser McKie*.
(http://www.frasermckie.com)

TEXTBOOK
3

National Curriculum Textbook 3

- This book covers every outcome of the Year 3 course, as laid out in the National Curriculum England framework document, (September 2013).

- There are no A and B exercises. The book covers the entire Year 3 course without the teacher having to pick and choose which questions to leave out and which exercises are important. They all are !

- The book follows on directly from TeeJay's Year 2 Books and includes revision and consolidation of the work covered in the Year 2 course.

- The Year 3 Book contains a 12 page "Chapter Zero" which primarily revises every topic from the Year 2 course and can be used as a diagnostic tool. This could be followed by TeeJay's diagnostic assessments* of the work covered in our Year 2 books.

- It also contains a Chapter 19 which revises every topic from the Year 3 course, prior to an end of year assessment.

- Non-calculator skills are emphasised and encouraged throughout the book.

- Each chapter will have a "Revisit - Review - Revise" exercise as a summary.

- Homework*, mirroring exercise by exercise, the topics in this book, is available as a photocopiable pack.

- TeeJay's Assessment Pack* for Year 3 work, is also available as a photocopiable pack, and can be used topic by topic or combined to form a series of Year 3 Cumulative Tests. It also contains a series of longer assessments covering the Outcomes as laid out in the National Curriculum England framework document (Sept 2013).

We make no apologies for the multiplicity of colours used throughout the book, both for text and in diagrams - we feel it helps brighten up the pages !!

T Strang, J Geddes, J Cairns

(March 2014)

* Available for purchase separately.

Contents

1. Write down all the missing numbers :-

   a   20   22   24   26   34   .... .

   b   85   80   75   55   .... .

2. What is the number just **down** from 80 ?

3. What is the number **two** up from 59 ?

4. What numbers do arrows
   A and **B** point to ?

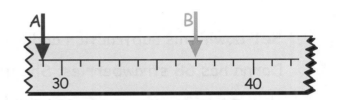

5. Copy and complete :-

   a   63
       + 6
   _____

   b   42
       + 35
   _____

   c   17
       + 61
   _____

   d   62
       + 24
   _____

6. Set **down** this sum and work out the answer :-

   Mary bakes **33** scones on Friday morning.

   She bakes **25 more** in the afternoon.

   How many scones did Mary bake on Friday ?

7. Do these additions **mentally** :-

   a   21 + 8   b   63 + 34   c   76 + 11   d   54 + 45.

8. *Work out the answer to this problem* **mentally** :-

   Sandra made some bakewell tarts for the church fete.

   She sold **71** of them. There were still **19** left.

   How many tarts had Sandra made ?

9. How many right angles can you see here?

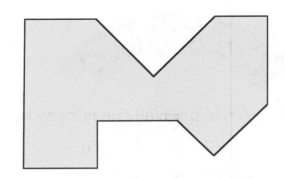

(*You may use an angle template*).

10. Copy and work out :-

a   57
   – 6
   ___

b   67
   – 25
   ___

c   88
   – 32
   ___

d   99
   – 61
   ___

11. **Set down** this subtraction and work out the answer :- Donna has **68** strawberries. She uses **55** to make jam. How many strawberries does she have left?

12. Do these **in your head** and write down the answers :-

a   16 – 11

b   77 – 23

c   97 – 44

d   85 – 25.

13. *Work out the answer to this problem* **mentally** :-
There are **86** sandwiches for sale in a supermarket.
13 of them are out of date on that day.
How many sandwiches will be safe to sell at the end of the day?

14. Write the following **heights** in order from **shortest** to **tallest** :-

tube train ,   cathedral,   chair ,   house,   hut.

15. Write these objects in order with the **least** volume first :-

lake,   sink,   tea pot,   wine glass,   pond,   bath.

16. Do these shapes or pictures have **symmetry** ? (Write Yes or No).

a

b

c

d

e

f

17. What are each of these 2 dimensional shapes called ?

a

b

c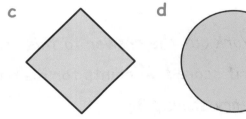

d

18. Name the **2 dimensional** shapes in the picture and say **how many** of them there are.

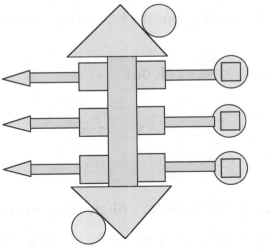

19. How many :-

a edges are in a circle

b angles are in a triangle

c corners are in a square

d edges are in a rectangle ?

20. How is a **circle** different from a **square** ? Give 2 answers.

21. Copy and complete :-

a   29
    + 7
   ─────

b   8
   + 75
   ─────

c   46
   + 28
   ─────

d   73
   + 19
   ─────

22. One box of matches contains 48 matches.

Another contains 49.

How many matches are there altogether ?

23. Do these additions in your head and write down the answers :-

a   17 + 8

b   54 + 28

c   76 + 19

d   35 + 47.

24. *Work out the answer to this problem mentally* :-

Arif scored 56 points for his basketball team.

Terry scored 38.

How many points have they scored altogether ?

25. Copy and work out :-

a   24
    - 7
   ─────

b   73
   - 28
   ─────

c   86
   - 19
   ─────

d   94
   - 36
   ─────

26. In good weather, Nick can clean 65 cars per week.

If it is a rainy week he cleans 18 cars fewer.

How many cars does he clean in a rainy week ?

27. Do these mentally :-

a   35 – 17

b   41 – 26

c   72 – 37

d   98 – 9.

28. *Work out the answer to this problem* mentally :-

This pencil case has 65 coloured pencils in it.

All 17 red pencils are removed.

How many pencils are left ?

29. List the notes and coins you might use to pay for each item exactly :-

   a

73p

   b

£2 and 37p

   c

£12 and 70p

30. Jo hands over a £10 note and gets the change shown.

How much did Jo spend ?

31. a Charles got £4 change from a £10 note.
      How much had he spent ?

    b Fiona got £12 and 40p change from a £20 note.
      How much had she spent ?

32. Write down the answer to :-

   a 5 x 2 = ...   b 8 x 2 = ...   c 4 x 2 = ...   d 6 x 2 = ...

   e 12 x 2 = ...   f 10 x 2 = ...   g 7 x 2 = ...   h 9 x 2 = ...

33. Copy and complete :-

   a   18   b   37   c   15   d   48
        x 2   x 2   x 2   x 2
        ———   ———   ———   ———

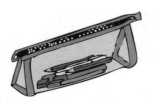

33. e   39   f   27   g   46   h   25
        x 2   x 2   x 2   x 2
      _____   _____   _____   _____

34. A cheap scented candle costs **47** pence.

     Nancy bought **2** of them.

     What did she pay ?

35. In this question, you have to choose from :-

Square - Rectangle - Rhombus - Kite - Parallelogram.

     (*Some questions may have more than 1 answer*).

     Which of the above shapes :-

     a   has **4** equal sides and all angles are right angles

     b   fits into its outline in exactly **4** ways

     c   has **no** line of symmetry

     d   does **not** have its opposite sides the same length

     e   has exactly **4** lines of symmetry

     f   can be made up of 2 triangles which are not the same size ?

36. a   Write the **days of the week**, beginning with **Sunday**.

     b   Write the **months of the year** beginning with **January**.

37. Write down the time on each clock **in 2 ways** :-
     (**Example** - *quarter past 7 or 7.15*).

     a   b   c

   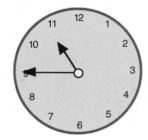   

38. Write down the answer to :-

    a   7 x 5 = ...   b   3 x 10 = ...   c   8 x 5 = ...   d   7 x 10 = ...

    e   9 x 5 = ...   f   5 x 12 = ...   g   11 x 5 = ...   h   9 x 10 = ...

39. Copy and complete :-

    a   16   b   39   c   8   d   19

        x 5   x 2   x 10   x 5

    e   14   f   48   g   27   h   12

        x 5   x 2   x 2   x 10

40. Novelty socks come in packs of 5.

    There are 18 packs for sale in a clothes store.

    How many socks is that ?

41.  Henry bought 7 nuts at 5 pence each,
12 screws at 2 pence each and
2 bolts at 10 pence each.

    How much did it cost him altogether ?

42. What 3-D shape is made up of :-

    a   2 circles and a rectangle   b   1 square and 4 triangles

    c   6 squares   d   2 triangles and three rectangles ?

43. How many :-

    a   faces has a cuboid

    b   edges has a cube

    c   corners has a triangular prism

    d   edges has a square pyramid ?

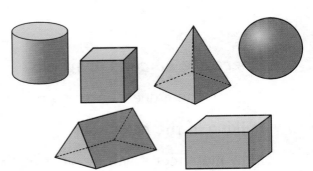

44. Find :-

   a   46 ÷ 2   b   35 ÷ 2   c   73 ÷ 2   d   95 ÷ 2

   e   2 ⟌ 28   f   2 ⟌ 70   g   2 ⟌ 93   h   2 ⟌ 69 .

45. Sonya buys **17** chews to be shared between her and her sister.
    How many will each girl get **and** how many will be left over ?

46. Find :-

   a   35 ÷ 5   b   40 ÷ 5   c   75 ÷ 5   d   82 ÷ 5

   e   70 ÷ 10   f   120 ÷ 10   g   91 ÷ 10   h   106 ÷ 10

   i   5 ⟌ 45   j   5 ⟌ 67   k   10 ⟌ 90   l   10 ⟌ 43 .

47. **Five pence** for a balloon.
    How many will I get for **95p** ?

48. What **fraction** of each shape is coloured here ?

   a   b   c   d

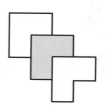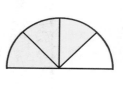

49. Trace or copy this arc shape.
    Colour in $\frac{1}{3}$ of the shape.

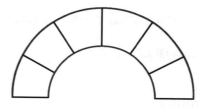

50. There are **28** cows in a field.
    $\frac{1}{4}$ of them are due to go in for
    milking in the next hour.

    How many cows will be **left** in the field ?

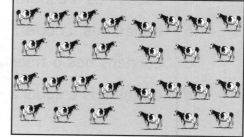

51. Ken uses the slabbed pathway on his garden to get over to his shed.

Describe his journey along the path.

(*Use turn left, turn right, forward*).

52. The fox is in the middle of the forest, looking at the chick.

a   If he makes a quarter turn clockwise what animal will he now be looking at ?

b   From his new position, he makes a half turn.

What is he facing now ?

c   From there, he makes a three quarter turn clockwise.

He is now facing an animal that has become popular on TV.

Which animal ?

53. Children in a Year 3 class were asked which meal they looked forward to most.

The table shows their answers.

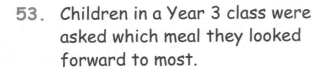 - stands for 3 children

Breakfast	
Lunch	
Dinner	
Supper	

a   Which was the most popular meal - how many chose it ?

b   How many more children voted for breakfast rather than supper ?

c   How many children were asked ?

54. REST-HERE offers cheap overnight stays as a special deal.

	Mon - Fri		Sat/Sun	
	Adult	Child	Adult	Child
Room Only	£26	£9	£30	£10
Bed & Breakfast	£35	£15	£40	£18

a   How much would it cost for one adult, **Room Only** on a **Thursday** ?

b   How much would it cost **in total** for Mr Jones and his son to stay for **Bed & Breakfast** on a **Saturday** ?

55. A group of girls in a cosmetic store were asked to name their favourite perfume. Their answers are shown in a block graph.

a   How many girls said YNDK ? (*not 2*)

b   How many in **total** for Kylo, Chloe and Vikki ?

c   How many **more** for Grada than Riod ?

d   How many girls were asked **altogether** ?

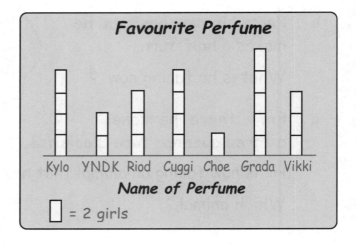

Favourite Perfume

Kylo YNDK Riod Cuggi Choe Grada Vikki

Name of Perfume

☐ = 2 girls

56. a   Measure each side of this rectangle to the nearest centimetre.

b   How much **longer** is the length than the width ?

57. Which would you use, (**cm** or **m**), to measure these :-

a   the depth of a swimming pool   b   the length of your pencil

c   the height of a bus   d   the width of a motorway ?

58. Find :-

a $\frac{1}{2}$ of 16p   b $\frac{1}{2}$ of 26 grams   c $\frac{1}{2}$ of £34.

59. What fractions are these arrows pointing to ?

a
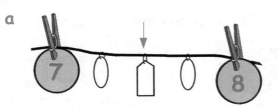

b
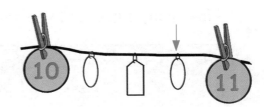

60. Copy this pattern and fill in the 3 missing fractions :-

6, $5\frac{3}{4}$, $5\frac{1}{2}$, $5\frac{1}{4}$,   5, $4\frac{3}{4}$, $4\frac{1}{2}$, ...   4, ..., ...

61. Do these examples in your head and write down your answers :-

a $7 \times 2 = ...$ b $45 \div 5 = ...$ c $56 + 23 = ...$

d $81 - 4 = ...$ e $27 \times 2 = ...$ f $5 \times 12 = ...$

62. Copy and complete :-

a   72
        - 25
       _____

b   78
        - 49
       _____

c   15
        × 2
       _____

d $5\overline{)85}$

e   18
        × 5
       _____

f $2\overline{)75}$.

63.

8p

14p

An ordinary candle costs 8 pence.

A Christmas candle costs 14 pence.

a   What will it cost me altogether for 5 ordinary candles and 2 Christmas candles ?

b   I have 80 pence to spend on them. How many pence will I have left ?

64. Use **tally marks** to show the number :-   a   9   b   27.

65. Use the given **key** to draw a **pictograph** showing the information which is in the table.

"How many times did you see a 3D film in a cinema last month"?

Donna	Sam	Anne	Paul	Tony
6	10	2	8	3

Key :-
stands for **2 times**.

66. The table below shows the number of slices of toast Gary had for breakfast over the past month.

4	2	3	3	2
3	1	2	1	2
1	2	1	4	3
2	1	2	2	3
4	2	3	1	2
1	4	1	2	1

Number	Tally Marks	How Many
1		
2		
3		
4		

a   Copy the table and use tally marks to complete it.

b   How many times did he only have one slice ?

c   How many days were there in this month ?

d   Draw a neat **block graph** from your table.

67. Would you use **kilograms** or **grams** to measure the weight of :-

a   a chicken drumstick   b   a ham joint ?

68. Would you use **millilitres** or **litres** to measure the volume of liquid in :-

a   a gravy boat   b   a hot tub ?

Hundreds, Tens and Units

Understand what each digit represents in a number.

Remember :-   62 is   6 tens and 2 units.

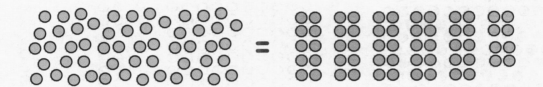

	tens units	
58 means	**5 8**	= **5** lots of **ten** and 8 units.

Exercise 1

Worksheet
1·1

1. Copy the picture
   and put in numbers
   and counters to finish it.

   =

   15   = ... **ten** and ..... units

2. Copy and fill in the boxes to make the correct number :-

   a 14 = [1] ten and [ ] units   b 26 = [ ] tens and [6] units

   c 37 = [ ] tens and [ ] units   d 81 = [ ] tens and [ ] unit

   e 63 = [ ] tens and [ ] units   f 90 = [ ] tens and [ ] units

   g 7 = [ ] tens and [ ] units   h 79 = [ ] tens and [ ] units.

3. I have 76 one pence coins. I want to put them in bundles of 10.

   a How many full bundles of 10 can I make ?

   b How many one pence coins will I have left over ?

4. A shop keeper bought 95 Easter eggs. He wants to put them on display with 10 eggs on each shelf.

    a   How many full shelves of 10 will he get ?

    b   How many eggs will be left to go on a smaller shelf ?

Numbers Bigger than 100

The picture shows how the number 125 can be split up.

	hundreds	tens	units	
125 means	1	2	5	= 1 lot of hundred, **2 lots of ten** and 5 units.

5. Copy and complete :- 237 = ... hundreds, ... tens and ..... units.

6. Write these numbers in hundreds, tens and units :-

    a   418 = ... hundreds, 1 ten and ... units.

    b   657 = ... hundreds, ... tens and ... units.

    c   902 = ... hundreds, ... tens and ... units.

    d   892 = ... hundreds, ... tens and ... units.

    e   760 = ... hundreds, ... tens and ... units.

7. Do the same with these numbers :-

    a   300   b   727   c   602   d   930

    e   275   f   384   g   717   h   989

    i   172   j   658   k   284   l   547.

8. How many £1 coins and 10p coins will you get for :-

a	340p	b	630p	c	960p
d	450p	e	880p	f	570p
g	500p	h	700p	i	1000p ?

9. Seven girls have some money.

How many 1p coins would each of them get ?

a   Anna   - £1 and 74p.

b   Beryl   - £2 and 48p.

c   Carol   - £6 and 20p.

d   Denise - £5 and 82p.

e   Evelyn - Four 10p coins and one 5p coin.

f   Fiona   - One £1 coin and eight 10p coins.

g   Gina   - Nine £1 coins, seven 10p coins and four 2p coins.

10. George goes to the newsagent and pays for his PC magazine.

He hands over the exact amount :-

four £1 coins

three 10p coins and

nine 1p coins.

How much did the magazine cost ?

11. Sarah's mum gives her six £1 coins, seven 10p coins
and five 1p coins to pay for a cinema ticket and popcorn.

How much does Sarah have ?

Place Value

A number can be written in **words** and in **digits**.
(A **digit** is a number like 1, 2, 3, 4, ...).

You should be able to change a number from one to the other.

Seven hundred and sixty three written using digits is 763.

524 written in words is five hundred and twenty four.

Seven hundred and sixty three
763 ✓

Exercise 2

1. Write the following numbers using **digits** :-

   a   twenty eight
   b   thirty eight
   c   forty five

   d   seventy one
   e   sixty seven
   f   fifty

   g   twelve
   h   eighty
   i   fifty nine.

2. Write the following numbers using **digits** :-

   a   one hundred and seventeen
   b   two hundred and forty three

   c   five hundred and sixty four
   d   three hundred and twenty six

   e   eight hundred and fifty five
   f   seven hundred and fourteen

   g   nine hundred and seventy
   h   six hundred and sixty seven

   i   eight hundred and eight
   j   nine hundred and ninety nine.

3. Write these numbers using **words** :-

   a   68
   b   42
   c   36
   d   18

   e   70
   f   95
   g   178
   h   319

   i   911
   j   504
   k   800
   l   1000.

4. Write the number that comes just before :-

   a 43   b 76   c 84   d 628

   e 951   f 640   g 790   h 800.

5. Write the number that comes just after :-

   a 34   b 88   c 49   d 109

   e 876   f 698   g 620   h 999.

6. Write the number that comes 10 after :-

   a 50   b 110   c 185   d 205

   e 290   f 513   g 794   h 991.

7. Write the number that comes 10 before :-

   a 90   b 140   c 195   d 310

   e 435   f 553   g 805   h 901.

8. Write the number that comes 100 after :-

   a 200   b 350   c 420   d 495

   e 501   f 756   g 890   h 900.

9. Write the number that comes 100 before :-

   a 300   b 250   c 390   d 450

   e 620   f 695   g 810   h 1000.

10. In a marathon race, Bob did well to finish in position 419.

    Joe finished the race 10 places behind Bob.

    What was Joe's position ?

Worksheet 1·2

11. Put each group of numbers in order. Start with the highest number :-

   a 302, 297, 453, 511, 388   b 452, 175, 234, 428, 301

   c 703, 578, 857, 519, 800   d 265, 256, 526, 625, 562.

12. Put each group of numbers in order. Start with the smallest number. :-

   a 17, 23, 31, 16   b 85, 72, 77, 81, 90

   c 106, 165, 172, 140, 114   d 581, 295, 259, 499, 501

   e 357, 430, 330, 389, 403   f 576, 657, 756, 567, 675.

13. An oak tree is aged 95.   An elm tree is 101.   A poplar is 87.

   A beech tree is 99.   A rowan tree is 104.   A willow is 94.

   Which tree is :-

   a the youngest   b the oldest

   c the second youngest   d the third oldest ?

14. What numbers are the arrows pointing to ?

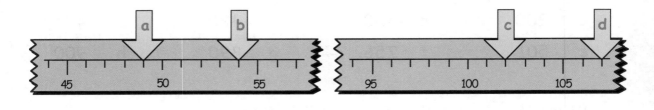

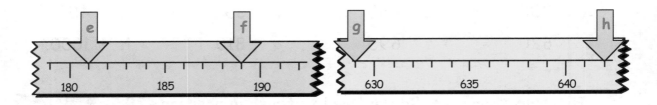

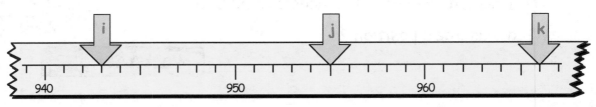

15. What readings are shown on these meters ?

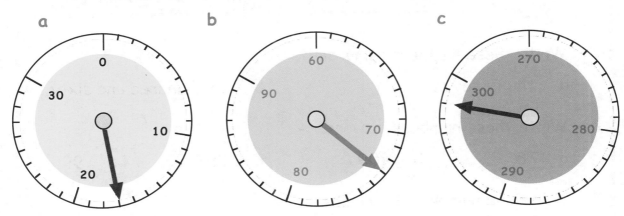

a   b   c

16. Seven hundred and twenty six people attended a gig starring Paul McCourtney at the G2 in London.

Write this number using digits.

17. A housing estate has 607 houses in it.

Write this number in words.

18. Write the answers to these in words :-

a   Derek tried the long jump.

420   430

centimetres

How far did he jump ?

b   How heavy is the TV ?

40   50

kilograms

1. Write these numbers using digits :-

   a   thirty seven   b   one hundred and sixty two.

2. Write these numbers in words :-

   a   78   b   409   c   753   d   999.

3. Write the number that comes :-

   a   just after 149   b   just before 800   c   ten after 390.

4. Put these numbers in order, starting with the smallest :-

   229,   188,   282,   314,   179,   220.

5. What numbers do the arrows point to ?

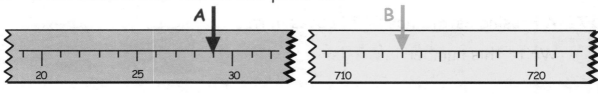

6. Bobby got 5 new £10 bank notes, all in order starting at NUMBER *000 711*.

   a   What was the highest number on his notes ?

   Bobby's sister, Fran, got two new £10 notes just before Bobby.

   b   What was the lower number on her notes ?

7. Jay, Ian and Ger are in a Javelin throwing competition.

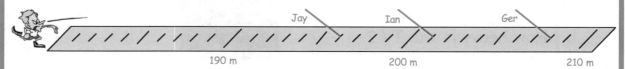

   a   How far has Ger thrown ?   b   How far has Jay thrown ?

   c   How much further has Ian thrown than Jay ?

Chapter 2

Angles

Smaller/Bigger than a Right Angle

Be able to identify a right angle.

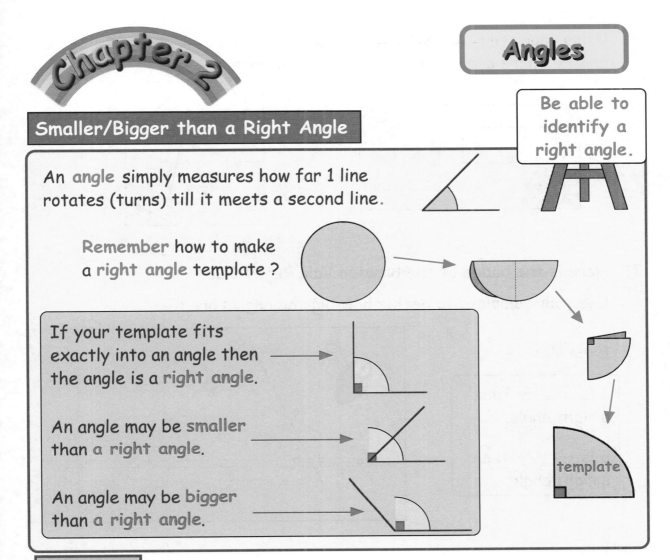

An angle simply measures how far 1 line rotates (turns) till it meets a second line.

Remember how to make a right angle template ?

If your template fits exactly into an angle then the angle is a right angle.

An angle may be smaller than a right angle.

An angle may be bigger than a right angle.

template

Exercise 1

1. Use your template to find out which angle is a right angle, smaller than a right angle or bigger than a right angle :-

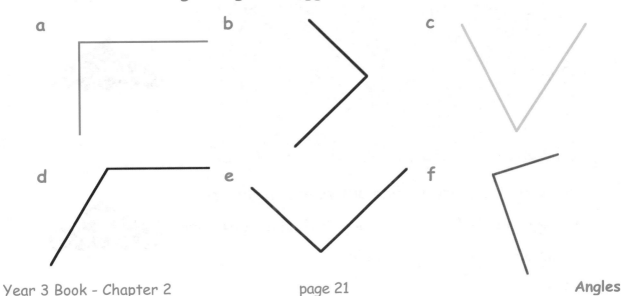

a   b   c

d   e   f

2. Using your template, write down how many **right angles** there are in the figures shown below :-

a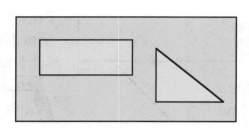

b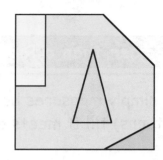

3. Here is the badge of the Newton Vale Rugby Club.

   Use your template to decide how big the angles are :-

   Examples :-

   > a is smaller than a right angle.
   >
   > b is .... than a right angle.

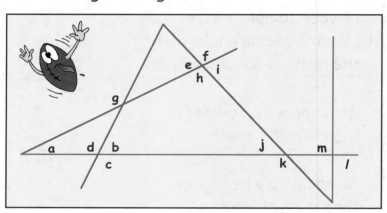

4. Steve potted the pink ball into a centre pocket in a game of snooker.

   The path the ball took showed how lucky Steve was to pot the ball.

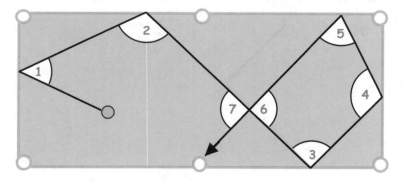

Use your template to find out which angles are :-

a right angled   b   bigger than a right angle

c smaller than a right angle.

Acute and Obtuse Angles

Be able to identify an acute or obtuse angle.

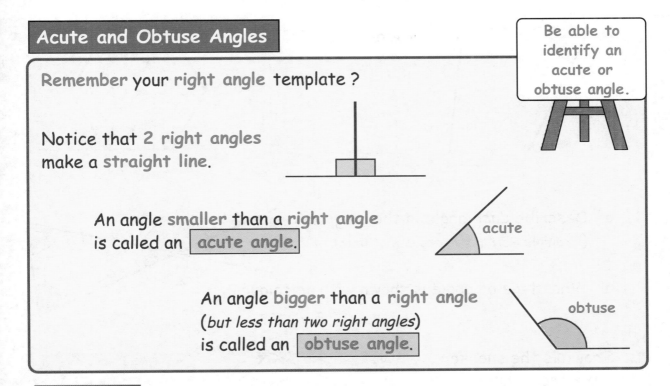

Remember your right angle template ?

Notice that 2 right angles make a straight line.

An angle smaller than a right angle is called an acute angle.

acute

An angle bigger than a right angle (*but less than two right angles*) is called an obtuse angle.

obtuse

Exercise 2

1. State whether these angles are right, acute or obtuse :-

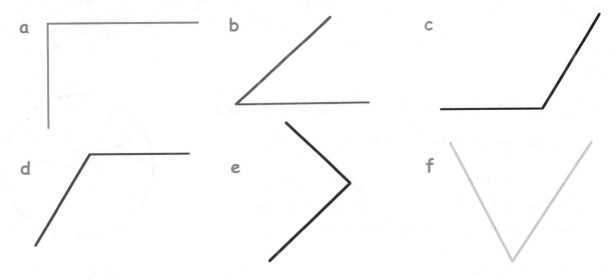

a

b

c

d

e

f

2. What type of angle is marked in each of these shapes ?

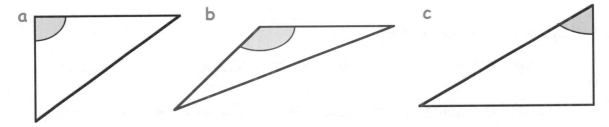

a

b

c

2. d 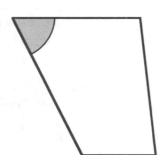 e  f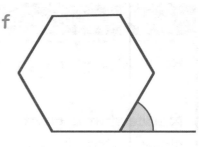

3. a Describe each angle in the diagram :-
      (**Example** - *the blue angle is obtuse*).

   b What type of angle is shown with **no** colour ?

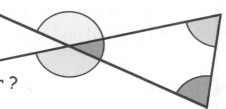

4. Shown is the snooker table from earlier.

   State whether angles 1 to 7 are **right**, **acute** or **obtuse**.

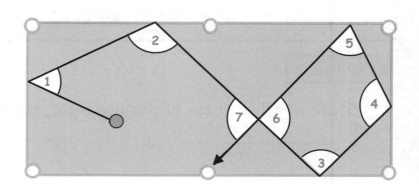

5. The time shown on this clock face is 10 to 3.

   The angle between the hands is **obtuse**.

   Describe the size of the (smaller) angle between the hands of a clock when the clock shows the following times :-

   a three o'clock   b five o'clock   c half past five

   d quarter past one   e eleven o'clock   f half past one.

6. Draw some examples of :-

   a right angles   b acute angles   c obtuse angles.

7. Find out the name for an angle which is **bigger** than **two right angles**.

Quarter turn, Half turn and Complete turn

Be able to identify quarter, half and full turns.

As the minute hand of a clock moves from the **12** round to the **3** it turns through a **right angle**.

This is known as a **quarter turn**.

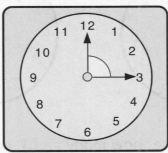

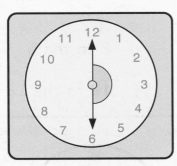

As the minute hand of a clock moves from the **12** round to the **6** it sweeps through **2 right angles**.

This is known as a **half turn**.

As the minute hand of a clock moves from the **12** right round to the **12** again it turns through **4 right angles**.

This is known as a **complete turn**.

or **one whole revolution**.

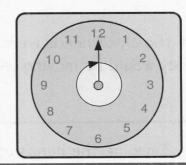

Exercise 3

1. How many **right angles** are there in a :-

    a quarter turn   b half turn   c complete turn ?

2. How many **right angles** does the minute hand move through on these clock faces ?

    a   b   c

2. d  e f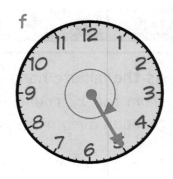

3. On a clock face, how many right angles does the minute hand sweep through when it moves clockwise from the :-

    a 6 round to the 9   b 7 round to the 1   c 2 to the 5

    d 3 to the 12   e 5 to the 8   f 12 to the 12 ?

The hands of a clock move clockwise.

If the clock hands were moving backwards they would be moving anticlockwise.

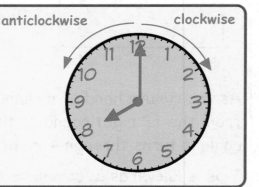

4. Imagine the hands of a special clock move anticlockwise.

    How many right angles does the hand sweep through when it moves anticlockwise from the :-

    a 9 round to the 6   b 7 round to the 1   c 2 to the 5

    d 3 to the 12   e 5 to the 8   f 8 to the 5 ?

5. If the minute hand moves from the 3 to the 6, it can do so by moving

    a quarter turn clockwise or a three quarter turn anticlockwise.

    Describe similarly, in two ways, the movement of a hand from :-

    a 1 round to the 4   b 8 round to the 2   c 7 to the 7

    d 5 to the 2   e 11 to the 8   f 4 to the 7.

Vertical/Horizontal and Parallel Lines

To be able to use vocabulary vertical, horizontal and parallel.

A **vertical** line is a line going up and down.

Examples :-
- a flagpole is vertical
- the edge of a building is vertical
- a line drawn up and down this page will be considered as representing a **vertical** line.

Parallel lines are lines which never meet, (*like the tracks of a railway*).

A **horizontal** line is a line drawn across - (*level* - parallel to the ground).

Examples :-
- any line on the classroom floor is horizontal
- any line on the classroom ceiling is horizontal
- a line drawn left to right on this page will be considered as representing a **horizontal** line.

When a **vertical** line and a **horizontal** line meet, they do so at right angles - they are said to be **perpendicular**.

perpendicular lines

vertical

horizontal

Example :- the classroom wall and floor are **perpendicular**.

Exercise 4

1. Which of the lines below could be considered as being :-

   a vertical   b horizontal   c parallel   d perpendicular ?

A

B

E

C

D

F

2. a   Are the red sides of this rectangle
       parallel ?

   b   Are the **blue** sides of the rectangle
       parallel ?

   c   Is each red line perpendicular to each blue line ?

3. Are the opposite sides of every rectangle parallel ?

4. Name some other shapes where the opposite sides are parallel.

5. a   Make a list of places where you see lines that are parallel.

   b   List some places where you see two lines that are perpendicular.

6. This yellow cuboid has a set of
   4 parallel lines marked in red.

   How many other sets of parallel
   lines can you see in the cuboid ?

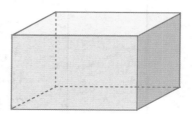

7. Look at each of the three dimensional shapes below :-

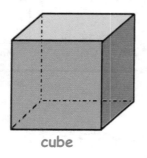 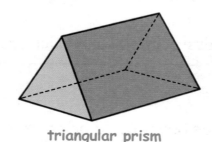 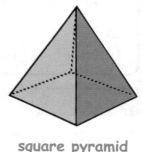

        cube   triangular prism   square pyramid

   a   How many sets of parallel lines are there in the cube ?

   b   How many sets of parallel lines are there in the triangular prism ?

   c   How many sets of parallel lines are there in the square pyramid ?

8. Investigate other 3 dimensional objects and find how many pairs
   of parallel lines and perpendicular lines they have.

Revisit - Review - Revise

1. State whether these angles are right, acute or obtuse :-

   a    b    c

2. State whether the angles 1 to 6 are right, acute or obtuse :-

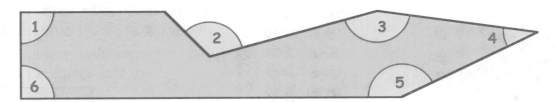

3. The time is 4 o'clock.

   Will the smaller angle between the hands of the clock be an acute angle, a right angle or an obtuse angle ?

4. Give an example of a time on a clock face which shows :-

   a a right angle   b an acute angle.

5. How many right angles are there in :-

   a a half turn   b a quarter turn   c a complete turn ?

6. How many right angles does the hour hand sweep through as it moves :-

   a clockwise from 3 to 6   b anticlockwise from 10 to 7 ?

7. Give a real life example of :-

   a a vertical line   b a horizontal line

   c a pair of parallel lines   d a pair of perpendicular lines.

Addition

Adding whole numbers up to 2 digits with no "carrying".

Addition   Revision

Example :- What's the answer to 31 + 23 ?

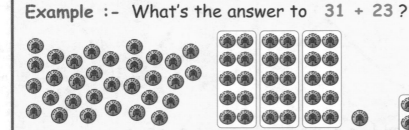

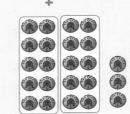

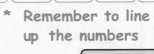

31 + 23 =

* Remember to line up the numbers

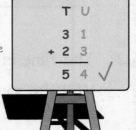

This can be written as

| 31 | + | 23 | = | 54 |

Exercise 1

1. Copy and complete :-

a   12   b   43   c   26   d   46
   + 11   + 14   + 13   + 43

e   51   f   87   g   47   h   73
   + 45   + 10   + 32   + 15

i   59   j   35   k   13   l   24
   + 40   + 24   + 56   + 71

2. Line up these sums, then work them out :-

  a   38 + 10   b   66 + 11   c   45 + 13   d   56 + 32

  e   33 + 66   f   22 + 11   g   41 + 5 + 23   h   41 + 22 + 4.

3. Len bought two garden hoses.

   One was of length 25 metres, the other, 40 metres.

   If he joins the hoses, what length will he have ?

4.

A butcher has 28 pork chops in stock, along with 51 lamb chops.

How many chops does he have in stock ?

5. In Greenpark Road, there are 33 houses on one side but only 24 houses on the other.

How many houses are there in Greenpark Road ?

6.

Richard and Fiona go strawberry picking.

Richard collects 51, but Fiona only gets 37.

How many strawberries altogether ?

7. A hardware store has 74 screw-in bulbs in stock.

   The shop also has 15 push-in bulbs for sale.

   What's the total number of bulbs ?

8.

There are three families of ants living in this ant hill.

One family has 20 members, another has 33 members, and a third family has 44 members.

How many ants altogether live in this ant hill ?

Adding whole numbers up to 2 digits with "carrying".

Example :- Add 39 + 53.

Set down like this :-

This can be written as

Tens Units (or ones)

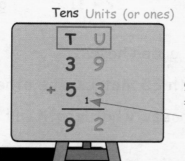

T	U
3	9
+ 5	3
9	2

9 + 3 = 12
= 2 units
carry 1 (ten)

39	+	53	=	92

* Remember to line up the numbers.

* Remember to add the numbers you have carried.

Exercise 2

1. Copy and complete :-

    a   57
        + 14

    b   46
        + 28

    c   35
        + 37

    d   29
        + 56

    e   25
        + 65

    f   61
        + 29

    g   77
        + 18

    h   42
        + 49

    i   31
        + 29

    j   65
        + 28

    k   48
        + 46

    l   33
        + 67

2. Line up these sums, then work them out :-

    a   38 + 55   b   47 + 37   c   25 + 25   d   29 + 58

    e   27 + 65   f   69 + 13   g   36 + 59   h   66 + 34

    i   88 + 11   j   22 + 39   k   41 + 5 + 38   l   10 + 52 + 8.

3. A fisherman caught **14** salmon and **29** trout when out fishing on the river.

   How many fish did he catch **altogether** ?

4.
   Lanna hides her pennies in two piggies.

   One piggy is full, with **75** pennies in it.

   The other piggy has just **17** pennies in it.

   How many pennies does Lanna have ?

5. Gerry pins up his **36** Christmas cards on the wall.

   On his birthday just after Christmas, he pins up his **28** birthday cards.

   How many cards **in total** are now on the wall ?

6.
   Eddie got his test marks back today.

   He got **27** answers correct and **19** wrong.

   How many questions were in the test ?

7. On a rainy Saturday, only **16** people were out on the golf course.

   When the sun shone on the Sunday, **66 more than that** went out to golf.

   a How many played on the Sunday ?

   b How many played **altogether** over the **weekend** ?

8. Freddie bought a newspaper for **35p** and rolls for **37p**.

   a How much did that cost him ?

   b He went back into the shop and bought an apple for **19p**.

   What was the **total** cost of the three items ?

Adding in Hundreds

Adding whole numbers up to 3 digits with no "carrying".

Example :- Do this sum 2 1 6 + 4 7 3.

Set down as shown.

* Remember to line up the numbers.

2 1 6 + 4 7 3 = 6 8 9

6 + 3 = 9 (units)

1 + 7 = 8 (tens)

2 + 4 = 6 (hundreds)

Exercise 3

1. Copy and complete :-

| a | 104
+ 3 | b | 429
+ 60 | c | 315
+ 34 | d | 426
+ 172 |

| e | 506
+ 391 | f | 572
+ 225 | g | 609
+ 140 | h | 681
+ 217 |

| i | 801
+ 177 | j | 856
+ 123 | k | 900
+ 87 | l | 637
+ 252 |

2. Line up each addition sum, then work out the answers :-

a 215 + 372   b 148 + 531   c 396 + 102   d 424 + 265

e 300 + 200   f 356 + 423   g 482 + 311   h 501 + 198

i 572 + 116   j 677 + 210   k 603 + 345   l 714 + 273

m 814 + 72   n 888 + 110   o 899 + 2   p 988 + 12.

Addition in Hundreds (with carrying)

Adding whole numbers up to 3 digits with "carrying".

Example :- Do this sum 3 2 8 + 2 9 7.

Set down like this :-

This can be written as

```
H  T  U
3  2  8
+2  9  7
  1    1
6  2  5
```

7 + 8 = 15
= **5** units
      carry **1** (ten)

1 + 9 + 2 = 12 (tens)
= **2** tens
   carry **1** (hundred)

3 2 8 + 2 9 7 = 6 2 5

* Remember to line up the numbers.

* Remember to add the numbers you have carried.

Exercise 4

1. Copy and complete :-

a   108
  + 135

b   437
  + 129

c   348
  + 442

d   666
  + 219

e   545
  + 376

f   397
  + 218

g   419
  + 492

h   688
  + 188

i   801
  + 109

j   444
  + 366

k   887
  + 99

l   999
  +   1

2. Line up each addition sum, then work out the answers :-

a   234 + 346   b   456 + 108   c   567 + 228   d   119 + 449

e   450 + 150   f   255 + 555   g   487 + 178   h   169 + 376

i   897 + 79   j   88 + 189   k   903 + 27   l   898 + 12.

3. Kenny earns £385 per week.

   Kerry gets £565 per week.

   What is their total wage ?

4.

   216 people are swimming at Leeds Baths.

   194 are at Bradford Baths.

   How many people are swimming altogether ?

5. Last year, John paid £567 for a holiday to Paris.

   He later spent £377 going to London.

   How much in total did he spend ?

6.

   In an orchard, there are 666 apple trees and 285 pear trees.

   How many fruit trees ?

7. Rena bought a table for £259 and two chairs for £258.

   a   Which was cheaper - the table or the chairs ?

   b   What was the total cost ?

   c   She also bought a rug for £99.

       How much did Rena spend altogether ?

8.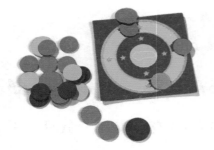

   Three children play a game.

   Yasmin scores 258 and 103.
   Trevor scores 177 and 192.
   Micky scores   304 and 179.

   The winner has the highest total score.

   Who won and what was his score ?

9. A laptop is on sale for £380.

    The printer costs £135.

    What is the total price ?

10.  256 people work in the Glynhall Hotel.

    The Firs Hotel has 175 workers.

    How many hotel workers altogether ?

11. There are 273 pages in a reading book
    and 648 pages in a store catalogue.

    How many pages in total are there ?

12.  498 seagulls are nesting on a cliff.

    There are 193 puffins there too.

    How many birds are on the cliff ?

13. Jack has £2 and 65p and Jill has £4 and 56p.

    They both change their money into 1p pieces.

    a   How many pennies does Jack have ?

    b   How many pennies does Jill have ?

    c   How many pennies do they have altogether ?

14.  The teacher of Year 3 has 265
    coloured pencils to give out.

    The Year 4 teacher has 357.

    How many coloured pencils do they
    have in total ?

15. The penguins in a zoo ate 274 fish.

    The seals ate 426 fish.

    How many fish was that altogether ?

16.  There are 184 bees outside a hive.

    Inside, there are 437.

    How many bees are in or around the hive ?

17. Mrs Thomas has made 365 grams of jam
    and 235 grams of marmalade.

    How many grams in total is that ?

18.  Going on holiday, Sam travelled 270 km.

    Her journey home was 295 km.

    How far did Sam cover in the 2 journeys ?

19. Hal made a castle with lego bricks.

    He used 216 grey bricks and 389 red bricks.

    How many bricks did he use ?

20.  Jasmine has 3 jars of jelly beans.

    One jar has 152 beans.

    Another jar has 137 beans.

    The third jar has 144 beans.

    How many jelly beans will Jasmine have
    when she empties out the 3 jars ?

Adding any
numbers up
to 3 digits
- a mixture.

Exercise 5

1. Copy and complete :-

a   24
    + 5

b   8
   + 37

c   41
   + 56

d   54
   + 76

e   209
   + 18

f   48
  + 723

g   114
  + 368

h   559
  + 286

2. Find the answers to these sums after lining them up :-

a   47 + 99

b   106 + 392

c   11 + 899

d   875 + 105.

3. Arith scores 239 runs at cricket.

Erin scores 77.

What is their total number of runs ?

4.  In a shop window there are 35 gold bracelets and 84 gold necklaces.

How many pieces of jewellery altogether ?

5. Chef has 7 starters, 15 main courses and 6 puddings on his menu.

Line up the numbers and add to find the total number of choices.

6. Find the missing number :-

a   147 + ... = 314

b   365 – ...... = 78

c   ...... + 145 = 665

d   ...... – 456 = 128

e   800 – ...... = 274

f   856 – ...... + 123 = 542.

1. Copy and work out :-

a   27
   + 6
   ____

b   8
   + 49
   ____

c   69
   + 19
   ____

d   77
   + 53
   ____

e   143
   + 478
   _____

f   53
   + 619
   _____

g   483
   + 357
   _____

h   297
   + 616
   _____

2. Line them up and add :-

a   52 + 88   b   407 + 399   c   85 + 749   d   775 + 219.

3. This empty biscuit tin used to have
   63 Jeely Dodgers and 28 plain tea biscuits in it.

   How many biscuits were there in the tin ?

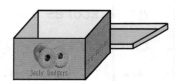

4. The reptile house in a zoo has just taken
   delivery of 163 lizards and 39 turtles.

   How many new reptiles is that ?

5.     Sandringham Kennels are selling
   boxer puppies for £297 and
   collie puppies for £185.

   What's the total cost for 1 of each ?

6. In November, a shop sold 167 copies of
   the computer game "Monkey Kong".

   In December, it sold 498 copies of the game.

   How many copies did it sell altogether ?

Chapter 4

| Analogue Clocks | Revision |

Exercise 1

1. a   Write the **days of the week** in order, starting with **Monday**.

    b   Write the **months of the year** in order, starting with **January**.

2. Imagine today is **Sunday**.

    a   What day of the week will **tomorrow** be ?

    b   What day of the week was it **yesterday** ?

3. Write the time shown on each clock :-

a   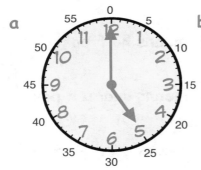   b   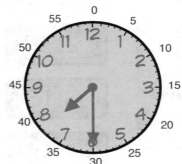   c

4. Write down the time on each clock **in 2 ways** :-
    (*Example* - *quarter past 8* or *8:15*)

a      b      c

5. List these times in order, starting with the **earliest** time :-

    5 o'clock,   5:05,   4:50,   quarter to five,   half past five,   4:40.

Be able to tell the time on a digital clock.

Remember :- There are 60 minutes in an hour.

Half Past is 30 minutes after the hour.

Quarter past is 15 minutes after the hour.

Quarter to is 15 minutes before the hour.

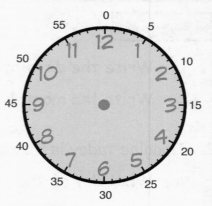

Digital clocks show the time using only numbers.

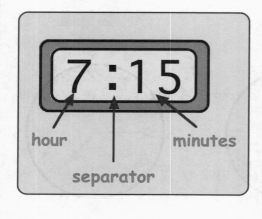

8:00	**means** 8 o'clock.
2:30	**means** half past 2.
6:15	**means** quarter past 6.
3:45	**means** quarter to 4.

45 minutes past 3 is the same as 15 minutes to 4.

Exercise 2

Worksheet 4·1

1.   Write the time shown on each clock using words :-

a   4:30
(half past ...)

b   5:15
(quarter past ...)

c   1:45
(quarter to ...)

d   8:30

e   9:00

f   6:45

1. g 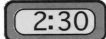 2:30　h 9:45　i 11:15

j 9:30　k 1:15　l 5:45

2. For each clock below, **draw** a **digital** clock to show the **same** time :–

a

5:1..

b

7:....

c

:

d

e

f

3. Write each time on a **digital** clock :–

a　half past 9　　b　quarter past 1　　c　quarter to 9

d　quarter past 3　　e　quarter to 12　　f　half past 2

g　quarter past 7　　h　quarter to 11　　i　half past 6.

Worksheet 4·2

| 2:25 |

The time shown here is twenty five minutes past two.

| 7:50 |

These clocks show fifty minutes past seven.

This reads better as ten minutes to eight.

4. Write the digital time for each of the following :-

Worksheet 4·3

a

b

c
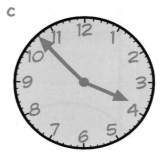

d	five past 3	e	ten past 12	f	twenty past 2
g	quarter to 7	h	half past 11	i	six forty
j	nine fifty five	k	eleven twenty	l	three thirty
m	five to 6	n	ten to 1	o	twenty to 4
p	twenty five to 1	q	one minute to 2	r	one minute to 8.

am and pm

Be able to interpret and tell the time using am or pm.

Each day is divided into 2 "halves".

> before – noon (ante meridian (am))
>
> after – noon (post meridian (pm))

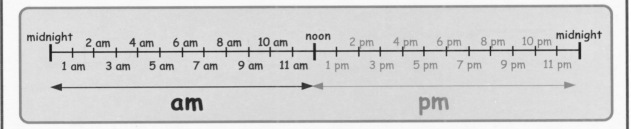

Most children start school at about 9·00 am.

Most people have their dinner at about 5·00 pm.

The clock time shown can be written in 2 ways

"$\frac{1}{4}$ past 8 at night" or "8·15 pm".

supper time

Exercise 3

1. Write down the time on each clock in 2 ways :-

a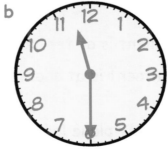

in the morning

b

just before lunch

c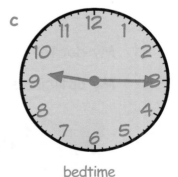

bedtime

d  3:30

school stops

e 6:20

wake up early

f 7:05

evening

1. g

Sunday morning

h

get up for school

i

asleep in your bed

j **6:50**

just after dinner

k **10:55**

morning break

l **1:15**

just after lunch

2. Write each of the following times using **am** or **pm** :-
   (*For example, "8·20 am" or "7·55 pm"*) :-

   a   Ben went to the cubs at $\frac{1}{4}$ **past six** last night.

   b    Zara watched a film after dinner which started
       at $\frac{1}{4}$ **to eight** and ended at **half past ten**.

   c   The Breakfast News started at **five past
       seven** and finished at **ten to eight**.

   d   My doctor's appointment is at **ten past one**.
       My optician's appointment is at **quarter past three**.

   e    My plane left Edinburgh airport this
       morning at **ten to seven** and arrived in
       London at **five to 8**. I then had breakfast.

   f   Jake left school at **twenty past three**.
       He arrived home at **twenty five to four**.

7:45 am	7:45 am can be written as "quarter to 8 in the morning".

3. Write each of the following times out fully :–
   (use "in the morning", "in the afternoon" or "at night")

a 2:30 pm

b 9:45 am

c 10:50 pm

d 7:52 pm

e 6:10 am

f 11:55 am

g
am

h
pm

i
am

j 3:41 pm

k 5:43 am

l 10:59 am

m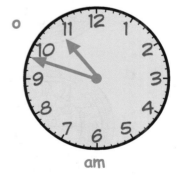
pm

n
am

o
am

p 1:11 pm

q 7:27 am

r 8:58 am

Clocks with Roman Numerals

Be able to interpret clock times with Roman Numerals.

The Romans had a different way of writing numbers.

They used a series of strokes to stand for 1, 2, 3, ...

Their numbering system went as follows :-

1 I	2 II	3 III	4 IV	5 V	6 VI
7 VII	8 VIII	9 IX	10 X	11 XI	12 XII

Discuss how the Roman numbers were formed.

You will often see Roman Numerals on clock or watch faces.

This clock shows four o'clock or 4:00.

This clock shows twenty to 6 or 5:40.

Exercise 4

1. Write down the time on each clock in 2 ways as above :-

a

b

c

d

e

f

2. Investigate how to continue writing Roman Numerals up to 20 or 100.

1. a   Write down the days of the week in order, starting with **Monday**.

    b   Write down the months of the year in order. Begin with **January**.

2. Write each of these times in 2 ways. (e.g. 1.40 or *twenty to two*)

a    b 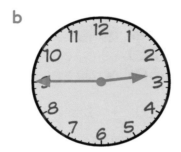   c

3. Write each of these times in **words** :-

a   5:15   b   8:05   c   9:55

4. Write each time below using **am** or **pm** :-

a    b    c   6:50

get up for school

Sunday breakfast   supper time

5. Write down these times in two different ways :-

    a   The long hand points to **VI**.
        The short hand points between **IX** and **X**.

    b   The minute hand points to **IX**.
        The hour hand is just before **VII**.

Subtraction

Subtraction with Carrying (or Exchange) Revision

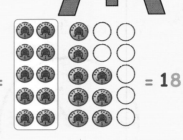

Subtracting a 1 digit number from a 2 digit number with "carrying".

Example :- What is 25 – 7 ?

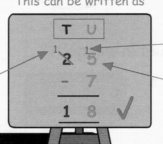

$$25 - 7 = 10 + 15 - 7 = 10 + 8 = 18$$

This can be written as

	T	U
	^{1}2	^{1}5
–		7
	1	8 ✓

We cannot take 7 away from 5.

We need to borrow (or carry) 1 ten and change this to 10 units.

This means the 5 becomes 15.

Then the 2 tens become 1 ten.
Now we can do the subtraction.

$$25 - 7 = 18$$

Exercise 1

1. **Copy** and **complete** these subtractions :– (You may use counters to help you)

a
$$\begin{array}{r} ^5\!\!\!\!\!\not6\,^1\!3 \\ -\ \ 4 \\ \hline \end{array}$$

b
$$\begin{array}{r} 32 \\ -\ 8 \\ \hline \end{array}$$

c
$$\begin{array}{r} 55 \\ -\ 7 \\ \hline \end{array}$$

d
$$\begin{array}{r} 25 \\ -\ 6 \\ \hline \end{array}$$

e
$$\begin{array}{r} 53 \\ -\ 5 \\ \hline \end{array}$$

f
$$\begin{array}{r} 84 \\ -\ 9 \\ \hline \end{array}$$

g
$$\begin{array}{r} 93 \\ -\ 5 \\ \hline \end{array}$$

h
$$\begin{array}{r} 80 \\ -\ 6 \\ \hline \end{array}$$

i
$$\begin{array}{r} 41 \\ -\ 2 \\ \hline \end{array}$$

j
$$\begin{array}{r} 63 \\ -\ 7 \\ \hline \end{array}$$

k
$$\begin{array}{r} 97 \\ -\ 8 \\ \hline \end{array}$$

l
$$\begin{array}{r} 100 \\ -\ 4 \\ \hline \end{array}$$

2. Set down the subtractions like Question 1 and work out :-

   a   45 – 7   b   60 – 3   c   72 – 5   d   38 – 9

   e   51 – 6   f   33 – 8   g   92 – 4   h   71 – 4.

3. There are **92** pages in Dave's book.

   In bed last night, he read the first **6** pages.

   How many pages to go ?

4. All **44** girls and **7** boys were rescued from a fire in a nursery.

   How many more girls than boys was that ?

5. **73** people came to the church coffee morning.

   Only **5** of them took sugar in their coffee or tea.

   How many people did not take sugar ?

6. Sally is doing her maths homework.

   Out of the **25** sums, she has managed to do **9**.

   How many sums is she stuck at ?

7. A baker sold **86** apple pies yesterday, compared with only **8** cherry pies.

   How many **fewer** cherry pies were sold ?

8. Jan splits a toffee bar into **30** pieces.

   She gives **11** pieces to Ann, **12** to Pat, and keeps the larger pieces for herself.

   How many larger pieces ?

Subtracting a 2 digit number from a 2 digit number with "carrying".

Example :-   Subtract **5**3 - 1**9**.

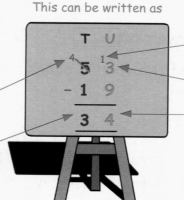

This can be written as

```
    T   U
   4   1
   5   3
 - 1   9
 ─────────
   3   4
```

We cannot take 9 away from 3.

We need to borrow (or carry) 1 ten and change this to 10 units.

So the 3 becomes 10 + 3 = 13.

9 away from 13 is 4.

Then the **5** tens become 4 tens.
Now we can do the subtraction.

1 ten away from 4 tens is 3 tens.

| 5 3 - 1 9 = 3 4 |

Exercise 2

1. Copy and complete :-

    a   ⁴5̶⁴ 4   b   42   c   64   d   73
         - 1 9   - 27   - 36   - 48
       _____   _____   _____   _____

    e   95   f   60   g   56   h   92
         - 25   - 12   - 29   - 34
       _____   _____   _____   _____

    i   85   j   74   k   97   l   80
         - 16   - 68   - 39   - 47
       _____   _____   _____   _____

2. Line up these subtractions, then work them out :-

    a   72 – 15   b   35 – 18   c   63 – 29   d   77 – 48

    e   50 – 36   f   61 – 33   g   86 – 57   h   91 – 62

    i   84 – 37   j   55 – 19   k   82 – 48   l   100 – 58.

3. A balloon seller makes 66 balloons.

    18 of them blow away in the wind.

    How many is he left with ?

4.

    Gareth Hale scored 41 goals last season.

    24 of them were from penalties.

    How many goals did he score which were not from penalties.

5. In the corner shop, there are 95 magazines left for sale.

    46 of them are about computers, the
    rest are on fashion.

    How many fashion magazines are on sale ?

6.

    The village chess club meets 52 times per year.

    There have been 34 meetings already.

    How many more meetings are still to be held this year ?

7. Kenneth has 83 pence left of his pocket money.

    He buys a new pen for 45 pence.

    a   How much money has he left ?

    He then buys an eraser for 19 pence.

    b   How much money has he got now ?

8.

    Bronte paid £91 for a set of 7 riding lessons.

    She had to cancel the last 3 lessons.

    She was given back £39 for her 3 lessons.

    How much had the first 4 lessons cost Bronte ?

Subtracting in Hundreds (no carrying)

Subtracting a 3 digit number from a 3 digit number, (with no carrying).

Example :- Try this **4 9 7 - 1 7 3**.

Set down as shown :-

* Remember to line up the numbers.

```
  H  T  U
   4  9  7
-  1  7  3
  ─────────
   3  2  4  ✓
```

7 - 3 = 4

9 - 7 = 2

4 - 1 = 3

$$4\ 9\ 7\ -\ 1\ 7\ 3\ =\ 3\ 2\ 4$$

Exercise 3

1. Copy and complete :-

a
```
   253
 - 132
 ─────
```

b
```
   369
 - 127
 ─────
```

c
```
   481
 - 301
 ─────
```

d
```
   436
 - 233
 ─────
```

e
```
   507
 - 205
 ─────
```

f
```
   572
 - 421
 ─────
```

g
```
   689
 - 314
 ─────
```

h
```
   697
 - 523
 ─────
```

i
```
   746
 - 214
 ─────
```

j
```
   879
 - 532
 ─────
```

k
```
   950
 - 450
 ─────
```

l
```
   999
 - 923
 ─────
```

2. Line up each subtraction before working out the answers :-

a   193 – 82   b   768 – 17   c   254 – 253   d   375 – 212

e   398 – 194   f   406 – 102   g   499 – 357   h   501 – 301

i   575 – 263   j   622 – 601   k   695 – 344   l   728 – 413

m   797 – 525   n   888 – 274   o   900 – 700   p   999 – 666.

Subtracting 3 digits from 3 digits with "carrying".

Example :- Try 7 4 6 - 1 5 9.

Your teacher will explain this.

This can be written as

We cannot take 9 away from 6.

We need to borrow (or carry) 1 ten and change this to 10 units.

=> the 6 becomes 10 + 6 = 16.

9 away from 16 is 7.

Then the 4 tens become 3 tens.

Now we can try to do the subtraction.

But we cannot take 5 away from 3.

We need to borrow (or carry) 1 hundred and change this to 10 tens.

=> the 3 becomes 10 + 3 = 13.

5 tens away from 13 tens is 8 tens.

```
  H   T   U
  6  ¹3  ¹1
  7̶   4̶   6
- 1   5   9
―――――――――――
  5   8   7
```

7 4 6 - 1 5 9 = 5 8 7

Then the 7 hundreds become 6 hundreds.

Now we can do the subtraction.

1 hundred away from 6 hundreds is 5 hundreds .

Exercise 4

1. Copy and complete :-

a   303
   - 124

b   431
   - 158

c   622
   - 187

d   710
   - 246

e   763
   - 294

f   397
   - 318

g   419
   - 275

h   725
   - 389

i   801
   - 488

j   834
   - 537

k   667
   - 89

l   912
   - 178

2. Line up each subtraction before working out the answers :-

a   834 – 547   b   856 – 592   c   961 – 635   d   802 – 687

e   903 – 705   f   830 – 764   g   900 – 816   h   926 – 878

i   807 – 371   j   800 – 408   k   903 – 59   l   1000 – 36.

3. Mrs Allen's jacket cost her £312.

   Her skirt cost £124.

   How much **dearer** was the jacket ?

4.  A holiday to Australia costs £805.

   A holiday to France costs £349.

   What's the **difference** in price ?

5. A large bottle of syrup holds **500 ml**.

   The smaller bottle holds **185 ml**.

   How many **more ml** is in the large bottle ?

6.  The chemist has a jar full of **510** flu tablets.

   Abbie buys **28** tablets from the chemist.

   How many are left ?

7. A secretary has **1000** envelopes.

   She has put stamps on **555** but has still to do the rest.

   How many has she still to do ?

8.  Farmer Bob has **823** haystacks to move over the weekend.

   On Saturday, he moves **595** of them and leaves the rest for Sunday - but he only manages to move **200**.

   How many are left to be moved next day ?

9. There are 312 tadpoles in a pond.

    221 have turned into frogs.

    How many tadpoles have still to change ?

10.  Out of 340 people asked, 50 said they did not like chicken curry.

    How many did like the curry ?

11. Mr Henderson gets paid £845 per week.

    Mr Peters gets paid £175 less.

    How much does Mr Peters get ?

12.  I drove 239 miles from home to Doncaster.

    Later, I drove 148 miles back up the road.

    How far had I still to go ?

13. Howard paid for 246 units of electricity in March.

    In January, he had paid for 518 units.

    How many units less did he pay for in March ?

14.  A plane was filled with 825 litres of fuel.

    It flew to its destination.

    On landing, there were 147 litres left.

    How much fuel had the plane used on its journey ?

15. A laptop is in a sale priced £435.

    A laser printer is on offer at £279.

    How much dearer is the laptop
    than the printer ?

16. Work out how much the sale price is :-

a
Normal Price = £45.

Sale Price = £ ?

£19 OFF !

b
£165 OFF !

Normal Price = £325.

Sale Price = £ ?

c
Normal Price = £190.

Sale Price = £ ?

£47 OFF !

d
£185 OFF !

Normal Price = £529.

Sale Price = £ ?

17. Work out how much I saved by buying in the sale :-

a
Normal Price = £135.
Sale Price = £93.

Saved = £ ?

b
Saved = £ ?

Normal Price = £925.

Sale Price = £539.

18.

£949

£949 - £450

£ ......

Ed Baines paid £949 for a 3D television.

His washing machine cost £450 less.

The vacuum cleaner he bought cost £175 less than the washing machine.

What was the price of the vacuum cleaner ?

Subtraction - A Mixture

Exercise 5

1. Copy and complete :-

a   83
   - 6
   ____

b   125
    - 9
   ____

c   74
   - 28
   ____

d   703
    - 91
   ____

e   81
   - 36
   ____

f   800
   - 235
   ____

g   724
   - 368
   ____

h   1000
   - 525
   ____

2. Line these up and try them :-

a   75 – 8

b   109 – 63

c   411 – 7

d   352 – 175

e   510 – 49

f   672 – 191

g   500 – 136

h   922 – 275.

3. Jordan has lived on a farm for 24 years.
   Mary has lived there for 7 years less.
   How long has Mary lived on the farm ?

4.  45 ordinary dustbins are ready for collection.

   There are 73 recycling bins there too.

   How many more recycling bins ?

5. Mr Samson's gas bill came to £212.
   Next door, Mr Watt's bill was £94.
   What's the difference in price ?

6.  Last year I paid £345 to get my car serviced !

   This year it cost me £189.

   How much cheaper was that ?

The 3 Я's

Revisit - Review - Revise

1. Work out :-

   a   62
        - 8
   _____

   b   415
        - 57
   _____

   c   647
      - 369
   _____

   d   701
      - 409
   _____

2. Find :-

   a   74 – 6   b   603 – 72   c   317 – 148   d   626 – 479.

3. There were 341 fashion shops in the area.

   Sadly 95 of them closed down last year.

   How many are left open ?

4.  There are two sizes of hose on sale in a garden centre - 35 metres and 16 metres.

   How much longer is one than the other ?

5. Sally sold £578 worth of cosmetics last weekend, compared to Hazel who sold £917 worth.

   How much less were Sally's sales ?

6.  Over the Christmas period, 534 puppies were sold.

   257 were spaniels and 169 were terriers,

   The rest were boxers.

   a   How many boxers were sold ?

   b   How many more spaniels than terriers ?

Chapter 6

Coins and Notes to £20 Revision

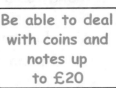

Money

Be able to deal
with coins and
notes up
to £20

Exercise 1

1. a   How many  are in ?

   b   How many are in ?

   c   How many  are in  ?

2. List the notes and coins you might use to pay for each item exactly :–

   a   b   c

     75p   99p   £1 and 80p

3. Daniel has    Simon has

   a   How much does each boy have ?

   b   How much do they have altogether ?

   c   (i)   Who has more money ?   (ii)   How much more ?

4. Pat and Peter have some money as shown.

Pat   Peter

   a   How much does Pat have ?

   b   How much does Peter have ?

   c   How much more does Pat have than Peter ?

5. Which notes and coins would you use to pay exactly for items costing :-

   a £7   b £16   c £28   d £55

   e £11 and 30p f £19 and 19p g £33 and 8p h £67 and 76p.

6. Alex hands over a £5 note and gets the change shown.

   How much did Alex spend ?

7. Sherry gave a £20 note and got this change.

   How much did Sherry spend ?

8. a Avi got £4 change from a £10 note. How much had he spent ?

   b Sonya got £8 and 50p change from a £20 note.
      How much had she spent ?

   c Katherine got £9 and 99p change from four £20 notes.
      How much had she spent ?

Notes and Coins up to £1000

Be able to deal
with larger
amounts of money
(up to £1000).

Previously we have used
£20, £10 and £5 notes
when buying goods.

When dealing with larger amounts of
money we could use a fifty pound note :-

Exercise 2

1. How much money does each person have ?

    a   Mr Johnson

    b   Mrs Johnson.

2. a   How much do the Johnsons have in total ?

    b   Who has more money, and how much more ?

3. List the notes you would need to buy something costing :-

    a   £125   b   £185   c   £260   d   £340

    e   £450   f   £675   g   £810   h   £1000.

4. Adam buys a new computer and hands over four £50 notes.

   His change is as shown.

   How much was his computer ?

5. Calculate how much each person spent :-

   a   Baz gives four £50 notes. His change is one £20 and one £10 note.

   b   Ellie gives five £50 notes. Her change is £23.

   c   Mr Finn is given £43 change. He used three £50 notes.

   d   Mrs Fry was given £27 and 50p change after handing over a £50 note.

6. For each of the following, calculate the change and list the notes and coins that could be given :-

   a   Sonny bought new headphones for £85.

       He gave the assistant two £50 notes.

   b   Li handed over three fifty pound notes for her £115 outfit.

   c   Jacob bought a new watch for £225. He gave five £50 notes.

   d   Annie paid £136 and 45p for her spa day.

       She handed over three £50 notes.

7. Gary gave eight £50 notes for his £354 and 99p plasma TV.

   He received the change shown.

   Is his change correct ?

8. a   How much money does each person have ?

Mr Smith

Mrs Smith.

Mrs Alik

Mr Alik

b   How much money do the men have altogether ?

c   How much money do the women have in total ?

d   How much **more** do the men have in total than the women ?

9. Look at the items below :-

Washing machine
£275

Microwave
£76

Carpet
£125

Use the Smith and Alik families from Question 8 to answer each of the following questions :-

a   Mr Alik buys the carpet. How much money does he have left ?

b   Does Mrs Smith have enough to buy the microwave ?

c   Which **family** has enough to buy the washing machine ?

9. d   Which two items can the Smith family afford to buy ?

    e   Do the Alik family have enough money to buy all three items ?

    f   The Alik family buy the washing machine and the carpet.

        How much money do they have left ?

10. Miss Merchant bought the following items for her car.

- 2 new tyres at £37 each

- 2 new window wipers at £17 each

- 2 car mats at £10 and 50p each

- A new registration plate costing £8 and 50p.

How much was her total bill ?

11. a   List these items in order (*cheapest to dearest*) :-

    laptop   2 litres milk   school shoes   school tie

    b   Estimate the price of each of these items.

    c   Find what each of these items actually cost.

12. a   Make a list of ten things that an adult might buy from a shop.

    b   Estimate what each item would cost.

    c   Find the actual price of each item on your list.

13. Discuss each of the following :-

    a   Why do you think most people do not carry a lot of money ?

    b   How do most people pay for larger items ?

Revisit - Review - Revise

1. a How many **10p** coins can I get for **£2** ?

   b How many **50p** coins can I get for **£5** ?

   c How many **£2** coins can I get for a **£50** note ?

2. List the coins or notes that you might pay for each of these **exactly** :-

   a

   78p

   b

   £16 and 75p

   c

   £77 and 30p

3. a Denzel gives a **£1** coin and gets **88p** change.

   How much did he spend ?

   b Mr Rigby hands over six **£2** coins and gets **£1** and **25p** change.

   How much did he spend ?

   c Ella gets **£5** and **20p** change from a **£20** note.

   How much did she spend ?

   d Sally hands over a **£50** note for her **£42** and **75p** dress.

   (i) How much change should she get ?

   (ii) List the coins she should get in her change.

4. Mrs Boyd has a bill to pay at the Beauty Shop.

   What is her total bill ?

   a new hairdo costing **£45**

   a jar of moisturiser at **£6** and **50p**

   a bottle of Shampoo at **£2** and **20p**.

Measure 1

Measure to the nearest Centimetre Revision

Be able to measure lengths to the nearest cm.

Exercise 1

1. a *Estimate* the length of each line to the **nearest centimetre** :-

    A —————————————————————

    B ———————————————

    C —————————

    D ————————————————————————

    b Measure and write down the length of each line above to the **nearest centimetre**.

    c Write down the length of the lines in order - **shortest** first.

2. a Measure the sides of this rectangle to the **nearest centimetre**.

    b Find the **total** distance around the rectangle, by adding.

3. Write down the unit, (**m** or **cm**, or **mm**), you would use to measure :-

    a the height of your house   b the length of a pencil

    c the width of a pencil   d the length of the classroom

    e the length of a fingernail   f around your head.

4. Write the following heights in order, from **tallest** to **shortest** :-

    teacher,   ceiling,   door,   desk,   bus,   myself.

Metres and Centimetres Revision

Metres (m)

Metres are used when measuring longer lengths.

A metre stick or tape or trundle wheel can be used.

Examples :-
- The length of the classroom
- The height of a building.

Centimetres (cm)

$1 \text{ metre} = 100 \text{ cm}$

Centimetres are used to measure small lengths.

Examples :-
- The length of your finger
- The width of this page.

1 cm

cm   10   20   30   40   50   60   70   80   90   100

1 metre

Measuring Millimetres

Be able to measure lengths to the nearest mm.

Millimetres (mm)

A ruler is used to measure in centimetres or millimetres.

A centimetre can be split into *10 equal parts*.

Each part is called a millimetre.

1 mm

0   1
cm

Millimetres are used to measure very small lengths.

$1 \text{ cm} = 10 \text{ mm}$

Examples :-
- The wire used in a paperclip is about 1 mm.
- The width of your fingernail is about 6 mm.

1. Write down the lengths (**in mm**) of each of these objects :-

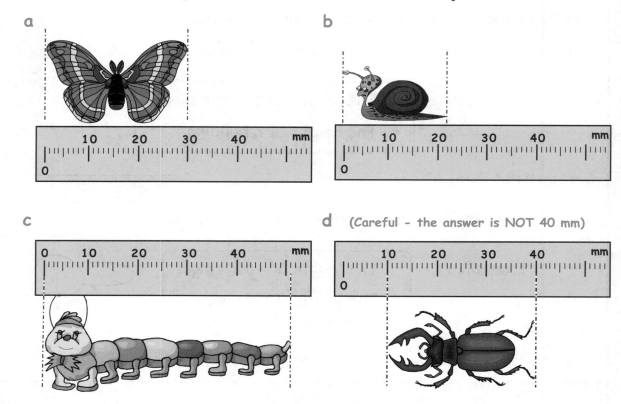

a

b

c

d (Careful - the answer is NOT 40 mm)

2. Write down the lengths of these lines (**in mm**) :-

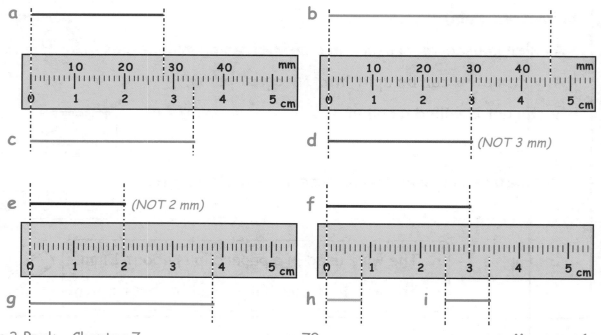

a

b

c

d (NOT 3 mm)

e (NOT 2 mm)

f

g

h

i

A ruler normally indicates the numbers only in cm (*see below*).

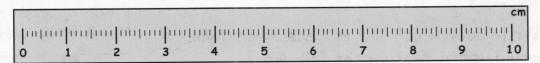

Remember that there are 10 mm in 1 cm, therefore :-

1 cm = 10 mm   2 cm = 20 mm   3 cm = 30 mm   4 cm = 40 mm .....

3. How many **millimetres** would there be in :-

   a   5 cm   b   7 cm   c   10 cm   d   6 cm

   e   half a centimetre   f   nine and a half cm ?

4. *Estimate* the length (**in millimetres**) of each line below, then measure the length (**in millimetres**) and write down your answers :-

   a _____   b

   c _____   d

   e _____   f _____

5.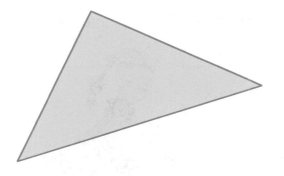

   Measure the three sides of this triangle in **millimetres**, and write down your answers.

6. a   Measure and write down the sizes of the four sides of this shape in **millimetres**.

   b   Calculate the **difference** between the longest and shortest sides.

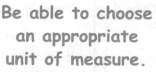

Be able to choose
an appropriate
unit of measure.

1. Write down which unit of measurement you
   would use to measure the following :-

   (*Choose between millimetres, centimetres & metres*).

   a The width of the classroom whiteboard

   b The distance from your classroom door
      to the next classroom door

   c The width of the top of a drawing pin

   d The length of a paint brush

   e The depth of this textbook

   f The length of a garden

   g The height of the nearest skyscraper building

   h The thickness of a coathanger wire.

2. What measuring device would you use to measure something in :-

   a millimetres (mm)   b centimetres (cm)   c metres (m).

3. Write down a list of things that you might measure using :-

   a millimetres (mm)   b centimetres (cm)   c metres (m).

4. Jeff measures the distance all
   the way round a badminton court
   (the perimeter) using a ruler.

   Sarah measures the same distance
   with a trundle wheel.

   Who is likely to get a more accurate
   measurement ? (*Give a reason*).

5. a Investigate different distances from one country to another.

   b Investigate what is meant by a light year.

Be able to find
the perimeter
of a basic shape.

The **perimeter** of a shape is simply :-

"the **total distance** around its outside".

This means you **add** all the
outside lengths together.

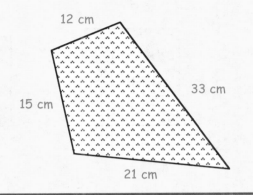

Perimeter = (12 + 15 + 21 + 33) cm

= **81 cm**

12 cm

33 cm

15 cm

21 cm

Exercise 4

1. Calculate the **perimeter** of this triangle.
   (*Show your working*).

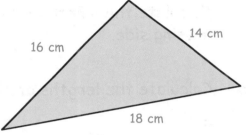

16 cm

14 cm

18 cm

2. Calculate the **perimeter** of each of the following shapes :-

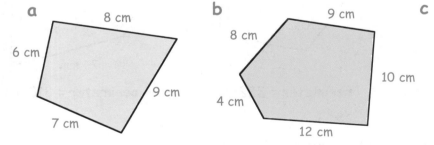

a

8 cm

6 cm

9 cm

7 cm

b

9 cm

8 cm

10 cm

4 cm

12 cm

c

49 m

62 m

71 m

55 m

37 m

3. Calculate the **perimeter**
   of this rectangle.

   (*Hint - it is not 18 cm + 5 cm*).

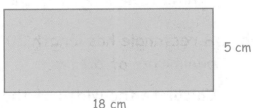

5 cm

18 cm

4. Calculate the **perimeter** of each of these rectangles :-

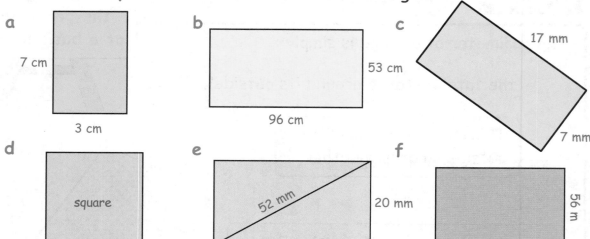

a
7 cm
3 cm

b
53 cm
96 cm

c
17 mm
7 mm

d
square
125 cm

e
52 mm
20 mm
48 mm

f
56 m
79 m

5. This triangle has a **perimeter** of **84** centimetres.

Calculate the length of the missing side.

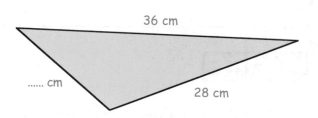

36 cm
...... cm
28 cm

6. Calculate the lengths of the missing sides of the following figures :-

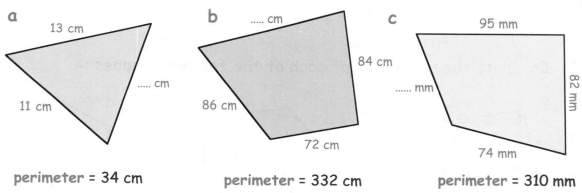

a
13 cm
...... cm
11 cm
perimeter = 34 cm

b
..... cm
84 cm
86 cm
72 cm
perimeter = 332 cm

c
95 mm
...... mm
82 mm
74 mm
perimeter = 310 mm

7. a   A square has a **perimeter** of **40 cm**.

What is the length of one side ?

b   A rectangle has length **20 cm** and **perimeter** of **50 cm**.

Calculate the width of the rectangle.

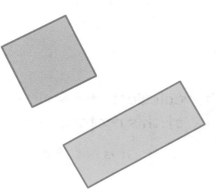

Drawing Lines and Shapes

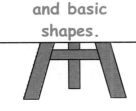

Be able to draw accurately lines and basic shapes.

1. Using a ruler, draw and label lines which measure :-

    a   4 cm   b   8 cm   c   12 cm

    d   20 mm   e   10 mm   f   45 mm

    g   87 mm   h   62 mm   i   122 mm.

2. Here is a sketch of a rectangle 8 cm by 3 cm.

    a   Make an accurate drawing of this rectangle.

    b   Draw a line from the top left corner to the bottom right corner (*a diagonal line*).

    c   Measure the length of this line in millimetres.

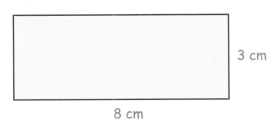

3 cm

8 cm

3. Draw accurately each of the shapes below :-

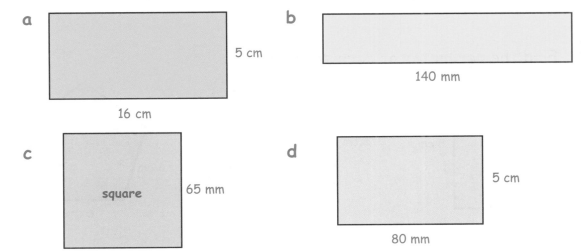

a

5 cm

16 cm

b

20 mm

140 mm

c

square

65 mm

d

5 cm

80 mm

4. Work out the perimeter of each shape in Question 3.

5. a   Draw accurately the right angled triangle shown.

    b   Measure the 3rd side and find the perimeter.

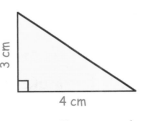

3 cm

4 cm

1. a   **Estimate** the length of each line in **millimetres** :-

     (i)   _____

     (ii)   _____

     (iii)   _____

    b   Use a ruler to measure each of the above lines.

2. Would you choose **metres**, **centimetres** or **millimetres** to measure :-

    a   the width of an airport runway

    b   the head of a screw

    c   the height of your TV screen ?

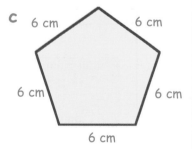

3. Write down the meaning of **perimeter**.

4. Find the **perimeter** of each shape below :-

 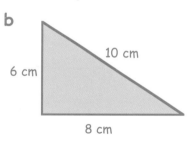

a   8 cm, 3 cm

b   10 cm, 6 cm, 8 cm

c   6 cm, 6 cm, 6 cm, 6 cm, 6 cm

5. Use a ruler to draw each of these lines (*label your lines*) :-

    a   5 cm   b   14 cm   c   34 mm.

6. a   Make an accurate sketch of a **square** with side 6 cm.

    b   Make an accurate sketch of a **rectangle** 7 cm by 20 mm.

Chapter 8

2-D and 3-D Shapes

Be able to recall some basic properties of 2-D and 3-D shapes.

Properties of 2-D and 3-D Shapes   Revision

Exercise 1

1.   Write down the name of each 2-D shape below :-

a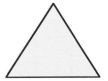

b

c

d

e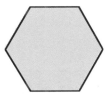

f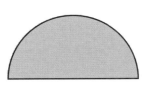

2.   Which of the above are symmetrical ? How many lines of symmetry ?

3.   Draw each of the following shapes accurately :-

a   a rectangle
     (7 cm by 4 cm)

b   a square
     (with side 6 cm)

c

9 cm

4 cm

4.   Write down the name of each 3-D shape below :-

a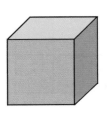

b

c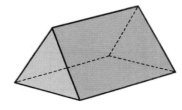

d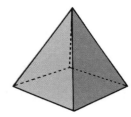

e

f

5.   a   What shape is each face in the 3-D figure in Question 4a ?

     b   Repeat for each 3-D shape in Questions 4b, c, d and e.

 Extension work

Be able to
identify a net
of a cube
or cuboid.

What is meant by the "Net" of a 3-D shape ?

The net of a cube is the 2-D shape you obtain
when the solid 3-D cube, made of cardboard,
is "opened up and laid out flat".

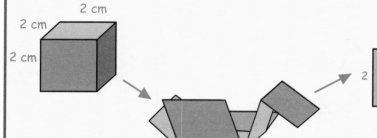

2 cm

2 cm

2 cm

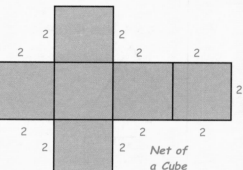

2

2   2

2   2   2

2   2

2   2   2

2   2   Net of
a Cube

2

- A cube consists of 6 faces.
- Each face is a square.

Worksheet 8·1

1. Shown below are 2-D shapes made up of 6 squares.

   For each one, decide if it is the net of a cube or not. (Yes or No).

a
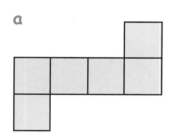

b
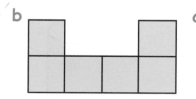

c
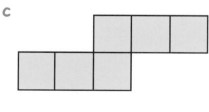

d
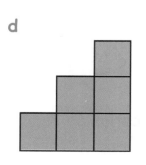

e
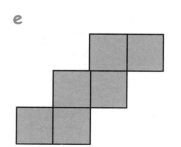

f
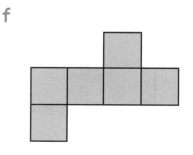

2. Investigate further nets of a cube, different from any of those found in Question 1.

3. Let us look at a special family of nets of cubes.

   Each starts with four squares in a row.

   a Decide on a simple rule where to put the other 2 squares so that you will always get the net of a cube.

   b Where would you not put the 2 squares if you wanted a cube net ?

Remember that a cuboid can be made from :-

4 rectangles and 2 squares **or** 6 rectangles

Worksheet 8·2

4. For each shape below, decide if it is the net of a cuboid or not. (Yes or No).

   a

   b

   c

   d

Extension work

Be able to identify the net of a 3-D Shape.

Most **3-D** shapes can be made from **2-D** shapes.

The net below can be folded up to make a triangular prism.

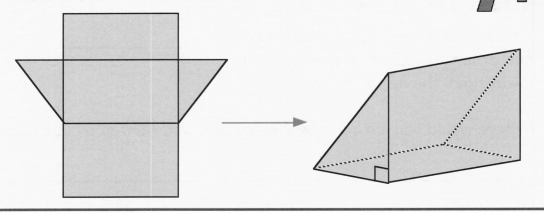

Exercise 3

Worksheet 8·3

1. Shown below are the nets of some **3-D** shapes.

    If each net below is folded correctly, write down the name of the **3-D** shape formed :-

a

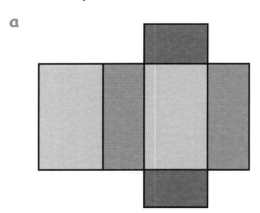

b

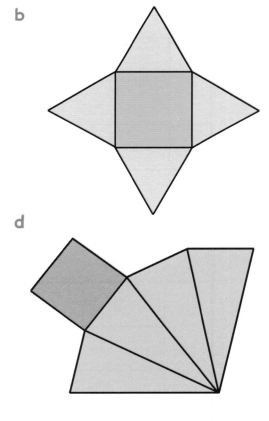

c

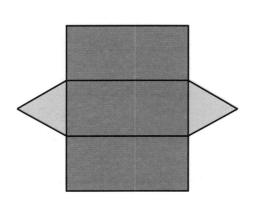

d

1. e 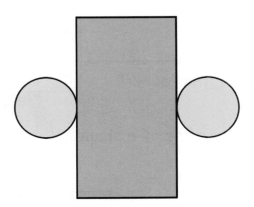 f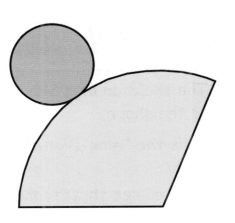

2. Which of the shapes below, if folded, could form
   a net of one of the main 3-D shapes we have met ?

a 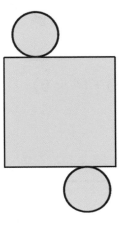 b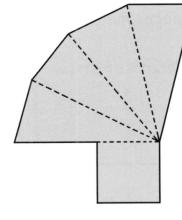

c 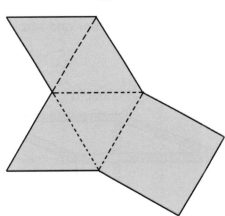 d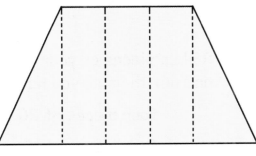

3. Try to make up your own net of a model house.
   (Hint:- think of what faces are needed
    and where they all should go).

4. Try to make some nets of
   your own of 3-D shapes.

Skeletons of Solids   Practical Work

The **skeleton** of a 3-D shape consists of the "bones" of the shape.

It is the "wire frame" that shows the outline of a shape.

Can you see that, to make the skeleton of this cuboid, we would need 12 straws ?

skeleton of a cuboid

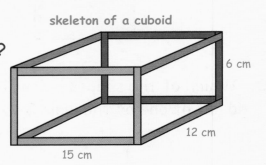

Four pieces measuring 15 cm.

Four pieces measuring 12 cm.

Four pieces measuring 6 cm.

Total length of straw = (4 x 15) + (4 x 12) + (4 x 6)

= 60 + 48 + 24

= **132 cm.**

Exercise 4   For this exercise, you are going to need **straws**, pipe cleaners or lots of pieces of **A4 plain paper** rolled into tubes, **scissors** and **sticky tape**.
(You may wish to work in groups).

1. a   Roll up pieces of your paper and cut them so you have :-

   • four pieces of 20 cm

   • four pieces of 15 cm

   • four pieces of 10 cm.

   b   Use sticky tape or blue tack to join the corners.

Cuboid

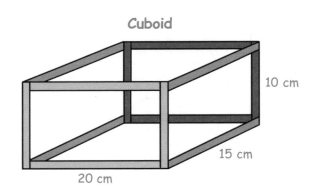

2. Make a skeleton model of a cuboid using :-

   a   4 pieces 30 cm long, 4 pieces 20 cm long and 4 pieces 15 cm long.

   b   4 pieces 24 cm long and **eight** pieces 16 cm long.

3. Make skeleton models of each of the following shapes :-
    (*You may be able to work in groups – ask your teacher*).

a

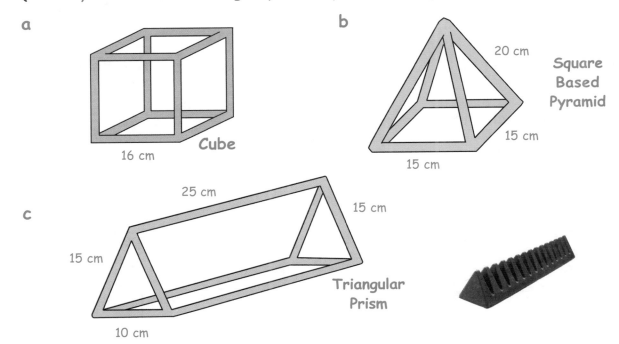

Cube
16 cm

b
20 cm
Square Based Pyramid
15 cm
15 cm

c
25 cm
15 cm
15 cm
Triangular Prism
10 cm

4. a Look at your cube in Question 3a.

    What is the **total length** of straw needed to make this cube ?

    b What is the **total length** of straw needed to make the square based pyramid in Question 3b ?

    c What is the **total length** of straw needed to make the triangular prism in Question 3c ?

5. a Use your straws to make this model tower.

    b What is the **total length of straw** needed to make this tower ?

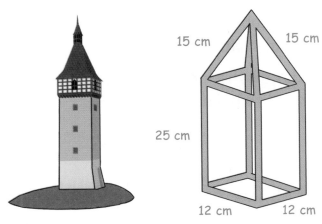

15 cm   15 cm

25 cm

12 cm   12 cm

6. **Investigate** making other skeleton 3-D shapes. (*For example - a house*).

1. Make a list of :- a five **2-D** shapes b five **3-D** shapes.

2. Draw each shape **accurately** :-

   a a square
   (*each side 8 cm*)

   b a rectangle
   (*3 cm by 5 cm*)

   c

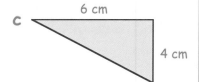

3. List the shapes you would need to build each **3-D** shape below :-

   a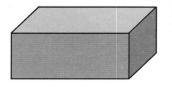

   b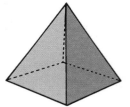

   c

4. Which of these shapes could be folded to make the net of a **cube** ?

   a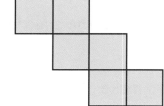

   b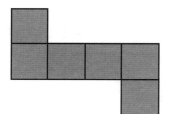

   c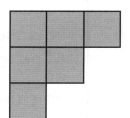

5. The cuboid shown is made from strips of metal.

   List all the lengths you would need to build this cuboid.

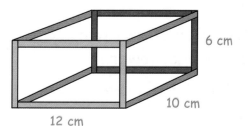

6. What is the **total** length of metal needed to build this triangular prism ?

Multiplication by 2, 5 and 10 Revision

Revise multiplying by 2, 5 and 10.

Exercise 1

1. Do these in your head and write down the answers :–

    a   2 x 6 =   b   5 x 4 =   c   10 x 7 =   d   2 x 8 =

    e   5 x 7 =   f   10 x 5 =   g   2 x 9 =   h   5 x 8 =

    i   10 x 9 =   j   2 x 10 =   k   5 x 12 =   l   10 x 11 = .

2. What numbers are missing ? (*do mentally*)

    a   2 x .... = 8   b   5 x .... = 10   c   10 x .... = 30   d   .... x 2 = 14

    e   .... x 5 = 30   f   .... x 10 = 40   g   2 x .... = 24   h   5 x .... = 55

    i   .... x 2 = 16   j   10 x .... = 90   k   5 x .... = 40   l   2 x .... = 18.

3. Copy and complete :–

    a   14   b   13   c   6   d   14
          x 2   x 5   x 10   x 5
        ──────   ──────   ──────   ──────

    e   15   f   28   g   8   h   43
          x 5   x 2   x 10   x 2
        ──────   ──────   ──────   ──────

    i   38   j   16   k   47   l   7
          x 2   x 5   x 2   x 10
        ──────   ──────   ──────   ──────

    m   19   n   50   o   12   p   17
          x 5   x 2   x 10   x 5
        ──────   ──────   ──────   ──────

4. A pack of cola has **28** cans.

    2 children are carrying a pack each.

    How many cans is that altogether ?

5.  Arthur sees his gran **5** times per week.

    How many times will he see her over a period of **14** weeks ?

6. James has **7** ten pence coins.

    How much money does he have ?

7.  A packet of cough sweets has **45** sweets.

    Daisy bought **2** packets.

    How many cough sweets did she have ?

8. Rodger drives **9** miles to the dump and **9** miles back home.

    He does this **5** times a week.

    How many miles does he cover in a week ?

9. 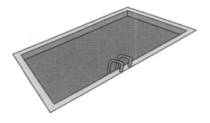 A swimming pool is **17** metres long.

    Joe swam **5** lengths of the pool.

    How many metres did he swim altogether ?

10. A chew costs **2** pence. A lolly costs **5** pence.

    A chocolate strawberry costs **10** pence.

    How much did Robert pay for :-

    15 chews + **6** lollies + **4** chocolate strawberries ?

Multiplication by 3

We have **3** sets of coins :-

 + + = = 3 lots of **1** coin = 3 coins.

We say $\boxed{1 \times 3 = 3}$

1 times 3 is 3

 + + =  = 3 lots of **2** coins = 6 coins.

We say $\boxed{2 \times 3 = 6}$

2 times 3 is 6

 + + =  = 3 lots of **3** coins = 9 coins.

We say $\boxed{3 \times 3 = 9}$

3 times 3 is 9

 + + =  = 3 lots of **4** coins = 12 coins.

We say $\boxed{4 \times 3 = 12}$

4 times 3 is 12

Again, the sign × is called the **multiply** or **times** sign.

When we write :- $\boxed{4 \times 3}$ we mean 3 lots of **4** which gives us **12**.

$\boxed{\text{We read this as} \quad 3 \text{ times } 4 \text{ equals } 12.}$

Use **coins** or **counters** to find out the following :-

3 lots of **5** coins, (5 × 3 = ?)	3 lots of **6** coins, (6 × 3 = ?)
3 lots of **7** coins, (7 × 3 = ?)	3 lots of **8** coins, (8 × 3 = ?)
3 lots of **9** coins, (9 × 3 = ?)	3 lots of **10** coins, (10 × 3 = ?)
3 lots of **11** coins, (11 × 3 = ?)	3 lots of **12** coins, (12 × 3 = ?)

1. **Copy** and **complete** :– *(For example, 1 x 3 = 3).*

   a   1 x 3 = ...   b   2 x 3 = ...   c   3 x 3 = ...

   d   4 x 3 = ...   e   5 x 3 = ...   f   6 x 3 = ...

   g   7 x 3 = ...   h   8 x 3 = ...   i   9 x 3 = ...

   j   10 x 3 = ...   k   11 x 3 = ...   l   12 x 3 = ...

2. **Write** out and **learn** the "three times table" by heart.

   Say to yourself, 1 x 3 = 3,   2 x 3 = 6,   3 x 3 = 9,   4 x 3 = 12,.....

   Practise it with someone **at home**.

   (Keep practising your "2 times table" and "5 times table" as well).

3. What numbers are **missing** ?

   a   .... x 3 = 9   b   .... x 3 = 18   c   .... x 3 = 21

   d   .... x 3 = 15   e   .... x 3 = 24   f   .... x 3 = 27

   g   .... x 3 = 30   h   .... x 3 = 0   i   .... x 3 = 36.

4. a   At dinner time each of the Reid family get **3** potatoes.

       If there are **5** people in the family,
       how many potatoes are used ?

   b   In a sponsored cycle event **3** boys each travel **7** miles.

       What is the **total** number of miles ?

   c   3 girls download **11** songs each.

       How many songs have been downloaded
       altogether ?

Be able to multiply a 2 digit number by 3.

We can **multiply** a 2 digit number (or **times it**) by 3.

Example 1 :- What is **8** 2 × 3 ?

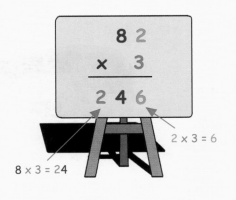

8 × 3 = 24

2 × 3 = 6

Example 2 :- Find **9** 8 × 3.

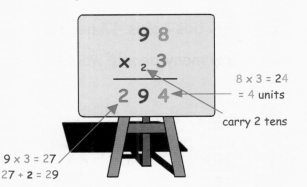

8 × 3 = 24
= 4 units

carry 2 tens

9 × 3 = 27
27 + 2 = 29

1. **Copy** and **complete** :-

a   14
    × 3
	b 25
	    × 3
		c 31
		    × 3
			d 42
			    × 3

e   92
    × 3
	f 73
	    × 3
		g 46
		    × 3
			h 53
			    × 3

i   57
    × 3
	j 89
	    × 3
		k 49
		    × 3
			l 65
			    × 3

2. Find :-

a   17 × 3   b   13 × 3   c   26 × 3   d   30 × 3

e   39 × 3   f   58 × 3   g   67 × 3   h   44 × 3

i   54 × 3   j   80 × 3   k   96 × 3   l   72 × 3.

3. a   A football team can have **25** players in their squad.

   How many players are there in **3** squads ?

   b   A pack of balloons costs **70p**.

   How much would **3** packs cost ?

   c   This bus holds **47** people.

   How many people would **3** buses hold ?

4.   A mixture   Find :-

a	52	b	84	c	31	d	75
	× 3		× 2		× 5		× 3

e	76	f	47	g	68	h	38
	× 2		× 5		× 3		× 5

i	97	j	94	k	96	l	77
	× 2		× 3		× 5		× 2

5.   **69** telephone poles have to be repaired.

   If it takes **2** hours to repair each one,
   how long will the whole job take ?

6.

3 people are playing darts
and each scores **87**.

What is their total score ?

7.   This jacket costs **£78**.

   If Ami is to buy one for herself and one for each
   of her two sisters, how much will it cost her ?

£78

Multiplication by 4

Be able to
multiply by 4.
Learn the
4 times table.

Hopefully, by now you can multiply by 2, 3, 5 and 10.

What we called the **3 times** table
looked like :-

      $3 \times 1 = 3$

      $3 \times 2 = 6$

      $3 \times \ldots = \ldots$

      etc

Multiplying by 4
(*the* **4 times** *table*)
can be done in a similar way.

Use 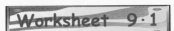 Worksheet 9·1

to complete the **4 times** table.

4 sets of 0 = 0	$0 \times 4 = 0$
4 sets of 1 = 4	$1 \times 4 = 4$
4 sets of 2 = 8	$2 \times 4 = 8$
4 sets of 3 = 12	$3 \times 4 = 12$
4 sets of 4 = 16	$4 \times 4 = 16$
4 sets of .. = ...	$5 \times 4 = 20$
4 sets of .. = ...	$6 \times 4 = \ldots$
4 sets of .. = ...	$7 \times 4 = \ldots$
4 sets of .. = ...	$8 \times .. = \ldots$
4 sets of .. = ...	$9 \times .. = \ldots$
4 sets of .. = ...	$10 \times .. = \ldots$
4 sets of .. = ...	$11 \times .. = \ldots$
4 sets of .. = ...	$12 \times .. = \ldots$

Exercise 4

1. Copy and complete :-

   a $4 \times 4 =$
         b $5 \times 4 =$
         c $3 \times 4 =$

   d $6 \times 4 =$
         e $9 \times 4 =$
         f $10 \times 4 =$

   g $7 \times 4 =$
         h $8 \times 4 =$
         i $12 \times 4 = .$

2. What numbers are **missing** ?

   a $\ldots \times 4 = 20$
         b $\ldots \times 4 = 8$
         c $\ldots \times 4 = 16$

   d $\ldots \times 4 = 28$
         e $\ldots \times 4 = 12$
         f $\ldots \times 4 = 36$

   g $\ldots \times 4 = 44$
         h $\ldots \times 4 = 0$
         i $\ldots \times 4 = 32.$

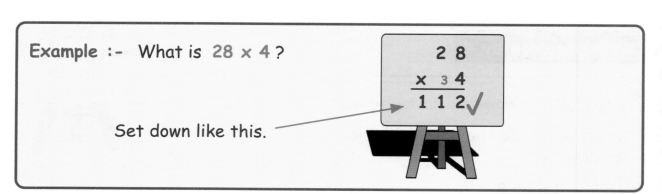

Example :- What is 28 x 4 ?

```
    2 8
  x ₃ 4
  1 1 2 ✓
```

Set down like this.

3. Copy and complete :-

a   14
     x 4

b   27
     x 4

c   43
     x 4

d   34
     x 4

e   52
     x 4

f   85
     x 4

g   38
     x 4

h   47
     x 4

i   70
     x 4

j   97
     x 4

k   89
     x 4

l   76
     x 4

4. Find :-

a   28 x 4

b   53 x 4

c   46 x 4

d   29 x 4

e   74 x 4

f   81 x 4

g   93 x 4

h   63 x 4

i   4 x 35

j   13 x 4

k   4 x 68

l   90 x 4.

5. a   There are 4 wheels on a car.

   How many wheels are there on 45 cars ?

b   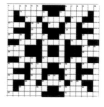 There are 19 words with 4 letters in a crossword.

    How many letters in total ?

c   Most taxis can carry 4 people.

   How many people can be carried by 37 taxis ?

Multiplication by 8

Be able to multiply by 8. Learn the 8 times table.

Now you can multiply by 2, 3, 4, 5 and 10 !

Multiplying by 8 (*the 8 times table*) can be done in a similar way to the others.

Use  **Worksheet 9·2**

to complete the 8 times table.

8 sets of 0	= 0
8 sets of 1	= 8
8 sets of 2	= 16
8 sets of 3	= 24
8 sets of 4	= 32
8 sets of ..	= ...
8 sets of ..	= ...
8 sets of ..	= ...
8 sets of ..	= ...
8 sets of ..	= ...
8 sets of ..	= ...
8 sets of ..	= ...
8 sets of ..	= ...

0×8	$= 0$
1×8	$= 8$
2×8	$= 16$
3×8	$= 24$
4×8	$= 32$
5×8	$= 40$
6×8	$= ...$
7×8	$= ...$
$8 \times ..$	$= ...$
$9 \times ..$	$= ...$
$10 \times ..$	$= ...$
$11 \times ..$	$= ...$
$12 \times ..$	$= ...$

Exercise 5

1. Copy and complete :–

   a $4 \times 8 =$
   b $2 \times 8 =$
   c $6 \times 8 =$

   d $5 \times 8 =$
   e $7 \times 8 =$
   f $8 \times 8 =$

   g $10 \times 8 =$
   h $9 \times 8 =$
   i $12 \times 8 = .$

2. What numbers are missing ?

   a $.... \times 8 = 48$
   b $.... \times 8 = 24$
   c $.... \times 8 = 0$

   d $.... \times 8 = 88$
   e $.... \times 8 = 32$
   f $.... \times 8 = 64$

   g $.... \times 8 = 56$
   h $.... \times 8 = 72$
   i $.... \times 8 = 80.$

3.

Sally's grandfather is 8 times her age.

If Sally is 7 years old, how old is grandfather ?

4. An elevator takes 5 seconds to go from one level to the next.

How long will it take to go from the ground floor to level 8 ?

5.

George gets £8 every week for his paper round.

How much does he earn for 4 weeks ?

6. Evelyn practices on her piano 8 hours a week.

Her concert is in 8 weeks time.

How many hours of practice will she have put in by then ?

7.

This tidy holds up to 10 items.

There is one tidy on each of the 8 tables in a classroom.

What is the greatest number of items they can hold altogether ?

8. Don bought pencils costing 8 pence each.

How much did he pay for a box of 6 ?

9.

Choc ice lollies come in boxes of nine.

Mr Magnum has 8 boxes in his freezer.

How many choc ices is that in total ?

Multiplying Two Digit Numbers by 8

Be able to multiply a 2 digit number by 8.

Example 1 :- Work out 51 × 8

```
  5 1
×   8
─────
4 0 8  ✓
```

Example 2 :- Find 8 × 67

```
  6 7
× ₅ 8
─────
5 3 6  ✓
```

Remember to "carry" the 5.

Exercise 6

1. Copy and complete :-

a	17 × 8	b	32 × 8	c	39 × 8	d	45 × 8
e	26 × 8	f	53 × 8	g	59 × 8	h	64 × 8
i	71 × 8	j	78 × 8	k	83 × 8	l	85 × 8
m	92 × 8	n	97 × 8	o	68 × 8	p	89 × 8

2. Set down and work out :-

a	13 × 8	b	25 × 8	c	37 × 8	d	28 × 8
e	44 × 8	f	52 × 8	g	58 × 8	h	40 × 8
i	8 × 79	j	8 × 86	k	8 × 99	l	62 × 8.

3. 8 children manage to get 30 sweets
    each from a large tin of toffees.

    How many toffees in total were in the tin ?

4.  Football tops are priced £42.

    Mrs Jones ruins 8 tops in her tumble drier
    and pops out to buy replacements.

    How much will she have to pay ?

5. It costs an ice cream seller 8p for
    each flake he puts in a 99 cone.

    If he buys in enough flakes for 75 cones,
    how much will it cost him ?

6. 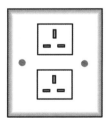 All the houses round where I live were
    built with 8 electric sockets in them.

    How many sockets were needed for
    all 88 houses ?

7. There are 8 seats in each row of an aircraft.

    How many seats will there be in a plane with 43 rows ?

8.  There are 36 tall ships in the harbour.

    I notice that each ship is displaying 8 flags.

    How many flags in total ?

9. An air freshener is set to puff out
    scent eight times in a day.

    If it lasts 57 days, how many times
    altogether will it have let out scent ?

Mixed Exercise

Be able to multiply up to 2 digits by 2, 3, 4, 5, 8 or 10.

Exercise 7

1. Do these in your head and write down the answers :–

    a   7 x 2 =   b   6 x 3 =   c   4 x 4 =   d   9 x 5 =

    e   7 x 8 =   f   9 x 2 =   g   8 x 3 =   h   7 x 4 =

    i   12 x 5 =   j   6 x 8 =   k   12 x 8 =   l   10 x 11 = .

2. What numbers are missing ? (*do mentally*)

    a   .... x 2 = 12   b   .... x 5 = 35   c   .... x 10 = 120 d   .... x 3 = 30

    e   .... x 4 = 36   f   .... x 8 = 64   g   8 x .... = 48   h   .... x 5 = 55

    i   .... x 2 = 16   j   4 x .... = 44   k   .... x 10 = 90   l   8 x .... = 56.

3. Copy and complete :–

    a   67   b   42   c   75   d   35
         x 2   x 3   x 4   x 8
    _____   _____   _____   _____

    e   87   f   68   g   37   h   88
         x 5   x 8   x 10   x 2
    _____   _____   _____   _____

    i   81   j   69   k   95   l   64
         x 4   x 3   x 2   x 5
    _____   _____   _____   _____

    m   55   n   73   o   80   p   77
         x 5   x 8   x 10   x 3
    _____   _____   _____   _____

4. Curry pies were on special offer in the bakers for **89p** each.

   Joe bought **2** of them.

   How many pence did he pay ?

5.  To carry out an experiment, a scientist used **75** jars, with **3** bugs in each jar.

   How many bugs did she use altogether ?

6. Each week, Millie puts **£47** worth of petrol into her mini.

   How much does she spend on petrol over **8** weeks ?

7.  Flo's Flowers sold **64** bunches of roses on Valentine's Day.

   If they cost **£5** per bunch, how much did the shop take in that day for roses ?

8. At Christmas, Joe the bin man got a **£10** tip from every one of the **36** house owners in my street.

   How much did he get in total ?

9.  These pencil cases can hold **58** pencils.

   How many pencils can **4** of them hold ?

10. A barrel holds **50** apples.

    5 greengrocers put in an order for **4** barrels each.

    How many single apples were ordered ?

Revisit - Review - Revise

1. **Copy** and **complete** :-

   a 3 x 4 =   b 5 x 4 =   c 7 x 8 =   d 6 x 10 =

   e 3 x 8 =   f 9 x 4 =   g 12 x 8 =   h 9 x 5 = .

2. **What numbers are missing ?**

   a .... x 3 = 27   b .... x 4 = 48   c .... x 8 = 88   d .... x 3 = 21

   e .... x 4 = 32   f 3 x .... = 36   g .... x 8 = 72   h 10 x .... = 90.

3. **Copy** and **complete** :-

   a   68   b   49   c   87   d   73
      x 2   x 3   x 4   x 5

   e   48   f   52   g   83   h   92
      x 8   x 10   x 4   x 8

4. Steak is selling at **£8** per kilo.

   How much will it cost for **8** kilos ?

5.

   These designer handbags are on sale at **£97** each.

   What would it cost for the **three** of them ?

6. Water tanks hold **4** litres of water.

   There are **12** trays of them stacked outside a factory and each tray has **8** tanks sitting on it.

   How many litres of water are there altogether ?

4 LITRES

Chapter 10

Measure 2

Looking back at using kilograms, grams, litres & millilitres.

Mass & Volume Revision

1. Put these vehicles in order of **mass**, starting with the **lightest** :-

Mini   Bike   Truck   Bulldozer   Motor Cycle

2. Which has the **greater** mass :-
   the pineapple or the two apples ?

3. 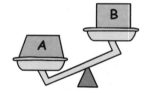 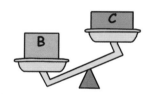   Which of the three boxes is the **heaviest** ?

4. Would you use **grams** or **kilograms** to measure the weight of :-

   a   your Christmas turkey

   b   a pack of butter

   c   an Easter egg

   d   a sack of potatoes ?

5. Which holds **less** water when full, a bath or a sink ?

Bath

Sink

6.

1 litre tin of paint

Watering can

Can of Diet Cola

Put these objects in order, starting with the one which holds the **most**.

7. Which takes up **less** space - a packet of breakfast cereal or a pot noodle ?

8. Put these in order, starting with the one which has the **largest** volume.

jug of water   eraser   golf ball   ice cream cone   microwave

9. Would you use **litres** or **millilitres** to measure the volume of :-

a   toffee in a Rolo

b   a barrel of oil

c   air in a hot air balloon

d   water in an egg cup ?

10. Andy has to take **2** allergy tablets **5** times per day in the summer.

He has bought **6** tubs of tablets **each** holding 20 tablets.

How many days will these tubs last Andy ?

Adding and Subtracting Mass

Be able to solve simple problems involving adding or subtracting mass.

Example 1 :-

A tin of soup has a mass of 328 grams.

A tin of baked beans has a mass of 234 grams.

What's the total mass of both ?

```
  3 2 8 grams
+ 2 3₁4 grams
  ───────────
  5 6 2 grams
  ───────────
    562 grams
```

Example 2 :-

Maida bought 2 kg 620 g of strawberries.

She used 1 kg 350 g to decorate a cake.

What mass of strawberries did she have left over ?

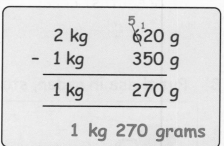

```
       2 kg   ⁵₁620 g
    -  1 kg     350 g
       ──────────────
       1 kg     270 g
       ──────────────
          1 kg 270 grams
```

Exercise 2

1. Copy and complete these additions and subtractions of mass :-

a	300 grams	b	680 grams	c	465 g
	+ 500 grams		– 240 grams		+ 348 g

d	2 kg 200 grams	e	6 kg 320 g	f	5 kg 175 g
	+ 1 kg 300 grams		– 2 kg 280 g		+ 2 kg 485 g

2. Set down as in Question 1 and work out :-

   a   270 g + 430 g

   b   418 g – 127 g

   c   1 kg 300 g + 4 kg 500 g

   d   3 kg 425 g – 2 kg 150 g

   e   3 kg 280 g + 6 kg 560 g

   f   7 kg 483 g – 3 kg 256 g.

Set down all working and work out the answers to these problems.

3. Cheryl bought in enough food for her friends to eat after a sleepover.

   a   What is the total mass of
       the buns and croissants ?

   b   What is the total mass of
       the muffins, the pancakes
       and the waffles ?

   c   What is the total mass of
       the butter and the jam ?

Here is what she bought.

Croissants	270 g
Buns	340 g
Muffins	430 g
Pancakes	315 g
Waffles	150 g
Butter	1 kg 200 g
Jam	710 g

4. Cheryl's mum had also been shopping.

   She bought 2 kilograms 800 grams
   of cherries to bake a cherry pie.

   She set aside 1 kilogram 750 grams of the cherries to make jam.

   How many grams of cherries were actually used in baking the pie ?

5.

   The postman delivered two parcels - one for
   Jan and one for her brother Danny.

   Jan's parcel weighed 4 kg 400 g and Danny's
   weighed 3 kg 250 g.

   a   How much heavier was Jan's parcel ?

   b   What was the total weight of the 2 parcels ?

6. Auldo the Bakers have 3 cakes in their window.

   Their total mass is 3 kg 995 g.

   The sultana sponge weighs 875 grams
   and the birthday cake weighs 1 kg 110 g.

   What is the weight of the chocolate cream cake ?

Adding and Subtracting Volume

Be able to solve simple problems involving adding or subtracting volume.

Example 1 :-

A bottle of juice holds 750 ml.

A paper cup only holds 180 ml.

What's the **total** volume in both ?

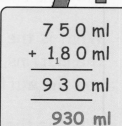

```
    7 5 0 ml
+ 1,8 0 ml
---------
    9 3 0 ml
---------
    930 ml
```

Example 2 :-

A kettle has 2 litres 500 ml of water in it.

A tea pot has 1 litre 120 ml in it.

What's the difference in volume between the two ?

```
            4 1
     2 L   500 ml
  -  1 L   120 ml
     ------------
     1 L   380 ml
     ------------
     1 L   380 ml
```

Exercise 3

1. **Copy** and **complete** these additions and subtractions of volume :-

    a   200 ml
       + 600 ml

    b   370 ml
       + 140 ml

    c   525 ml
       + 269 ml

    d   2 L 300 ml
      + 1 L 400 ml

    e   8 L 420 ml
      − 3 L 380 ml

    f   4 L 275 ml
      + 6 L 395 ml

2. **Set down** as in Question 1 and work out :-

    a   350 ml + 550 ml

    b   400 ml − 130 ml

    c   1 L 300 ml + 4 L 500 ml

    d   4 L 950 ml − 2 L 25 ml

    e   3 L 140 ml + 5 L 620 ml

    f   7 L 700 ml − 4 L 225 ml.

3. Derek sees 2 cartons of blueberry juice in the fridge.

   One has $\frac{3}{4}$ litre (750 ml) in it.

   The other has $\frac{1}{2}$ litre (500 ml) in it.

   What's the difference in volume ?

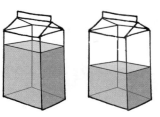

4.  Joe's indoor bath can hold 90 litres 380 ml.

   His outdoor hot tub can hold 200 litres 450 ml.

   How much water does it take to fill them both ?

5. Haunds Cream comes in three sizes.

   How many more ml does the largest jar hold than the smallest ?

   185 ml   250 ml   345 ml

6. 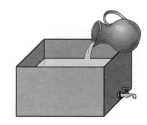 When full, the jug holds 3 litres 275 ml of water.

   The tank already has 12 litres 560 ml in it.

   How much will be in the tank when 1 jug of water is added ?

7. Kath has 14 litres 700 ml of rain water in her tank.

   She uses 2 buckets of water, each holding
   4 litres 50 ml, to water her garden plants.

   How much water is left in the tank ?

8. The washing machine holds 35 litres 590 ml of water.

   The dishwasher holds 17 litres 240 ml.

   How much water will both machines take in when they are on at the same time ?

1. **Copy** and **complete** these additions and subtractions :-

   a   250 grams
      + 350 grams

   b   720 ml
      – 370 ml

   c   7 kg 500 g
      + 3 kg 420 g

   d   8 L 630 ml
      + 4 L 280 ml

   e   10 kg 520 g
      – 3 kg 150 g

   f   5 L 700 ml
      – 2 L 315 ml

2. **Set down** as in Question 1 and work out :-

   a   350 grams + 550 grams

   b   800 ml – 390 ml

   c   2 kg 120 g + 6 kg 480 g

   d   4 L 650 ml + 5 L 75 ml

   e   10 L 540 ml – 4 L 170 ml

   f   17 kg 600 g – 12 kg 550 g.

3. Wheelie bins come in many sizes.

   The largest is a **660** litre bin. The smallest, **75** litres.

   Tony gets one of each size from the council.

   What's the total volume of his bins ?

4.     Ami buys **950 g** of raisins to make a fruit loaf and some scones.

   She uses **200** grams for the scones and then **650** grams for the fruit loaf.

   She keeps the rest to have with her breakfast cereal over the next **5** mornings.

   How many grams of raisins will she have with her cereal **each** morning ?

Revision of
dividing by 2,
5 and 10.

Division by 2, 5 and 10 Revision

Exercise 1

1. Do these **in your head** and write down the answers :–

    a   14 ÷ 2 =   b   20 ÷ 5 =   c   30 ÷ 10 =   d   18 ÷ 2 =

    e   45 ÷ 5 =   f   80 ÷ 10 =   g   19 ÷ 2 =   h   47 ÷ 5 =

    i   71 ÷ 10 =   j   25 ÷ 2 =   k   64 ÷ 5 =   l   111 ÷ 10 = .

2. What numbers are missing ? (*do mentally*)

    a   12 ÷ .... = 6   b   25 ÷ .... = 5   c   50 ÷ .... = 5   d   .... ÷ 2 = 24

    e   .... ÷ 5 = 20   f   .... ÷ 10 = 10   g   2 ÷ .... = 1   h   65 ÷ .... = 13

    i   50 ÷ .... = 10   j   .... ÷ 2 = 30   k   5 ÷ .... = 1   l   .... ÷ 10 = 0.

3. Copy and complete :–

    a $2\overline{)64}$ b $5\overline{)55}$ c $2\overline{)38}$ d $10\overline{)50}$

    e $5\overline{)80}$ f $2\overline{)76}$ g $5\overline{)95}$ h $10\overline{)30}$

    i $2\overline{)27}$ j $5\overline{)62}$ k $10\overline{)70}$ l $2\overline{)19}$

    m $2\overline{)73}$ n $5\overline{)83}$ o $10\overline{)96}$ p $5\overline{)17}$.

4. How many **5** centimetre pieces of ribbon can be cut from ribbon **45** centimetres long ?

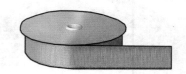

5.

Jack has **67** pence.

A chew costs **2** pence.

How many can he buy ?

6. Pork chops are sealed in packs of **2**.

How many packs are needed for **76** chops ?

7.

Cake trays hold **10** cup cakes.

I made **120** cakes.

How many trays did I fill ?

8. A recipe said I needed **70** ml of milk.

I only used **half** of that.

How many ml did I use ?

9.

A vegetable grower packs beetroot into packs of **10**.

She has **302** beetroot.

How many full packs will she get ?

10. **73** children turn up to play **5**-a-side football.

   a   How many teams can be formed ?

   b   How many **more** children are needed to make another team ?

Division by 3 (No Remainder)

Dividing by **3** is the same as sharing equally among **three**.

Flo has **3** apples.

She shares them with Jen and Anna.

Flo, Jen and Anna each get **1** apple.

We say that   3 divided by 3 = 1.

or   **3 ÷ 3 = 1**

this is the dividing sign

Ben has **6** doughnuts.

He shares them with Tom and Paul.

Ben, Tom and Paul each get **2** doughnuts.

We say that   6 divided by 3 = 2.

or   **6 ÷ 3 = 2**

Tom has **9** biscuits.

He shares them equally with Dick and Harry.

Tom, Dick and Harry each get **3** biscuits.

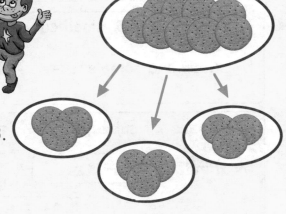

We say that   9 divided by 3 = 3.

or   **9 ÷ 3 = 3**

Exercise 2   You will need small counters here, or coins or cubes.
Possibly work in groups of 3 or on your own.

1. a   Count out 12 small counters (any colours).

   b   Share them equally among
   you and your 2 friends.

   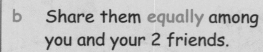
   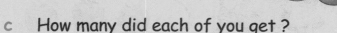

   c   How many did each of you get ?

   d   Copy and complete :-   12 divided by 3 = ... => $12 \div 3 = ...$

2. a   This time count out 15 small counters.

   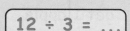

   b
   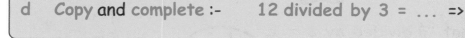
   Share them equally between
   you and your 2 friends.

   c   How many did each of you get ?

   d   Copy and complete :-   15 divided by 3 = ... => $15 \div 3 = ...$

3. a   This time count out 18 small counters.

   b   Share them equally again.   How many did each of you get ?

   c   Copy and complete :-   18 divided by 3 = ... => $18 \div 3 = ...$

4. a   Count out 21 small cubes and share them equally between you.

   b   Copy and complete :-   21 divided by 3 = ... => $21 \div 3 = ...$

5. a   Share 24 cubes, then 27, then 30, 33 and 36 cubes between you.

   b   Find :- $24 \div 3 = ...$ $27 \div 3 = ...$ $30 \div 3 = ...$
   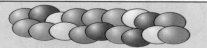
        $33 \div 3 = ...$ $36 \div 3 = ...$

1. Copy each of these and complete :-

   a   9 ÷ 3 = ...   b   6 ÷ 3 = ...   c   15 ÷ 3 = ...

   d   12 ÷ 3 = ...   e   18 ÷ 3 = ...   f   24 ÷ 3 = ...

   g   21 ÷ 3 = ...   h   27 ÷ 3 = ...   i   30 ÷ 3 = ...

2. Find the missing numbers :-

   a   ▢ ÷ 3 = 7   b   ◯ ÷ 3 = 3   c   △ ÷ 3 = 6

   d   △ ÷ 3 = 5   e   ▢ ÷ 3 = 8   f   ◯ ÷ 3 = 10.

3. Do these questions mentally :-

   a   6 allergy pills were shared equally between 3 gardeners.
       How many pills did each gardener get ?

   b   Dad ate the fish, but the 27 chips went to the 3 children.
       If they got the same amount, how many did each get ?

   c   A farmer put 18 scarecrows into 3 fields.
       Each field had the same number of scarecrows.
       How many were in each field ?

   d   I put 3 fruit sticks on to each melon.
       If I have 12 fruit sticks, how many melons will I need ?

   e   A menu gives a choice of 30 items of food.
       There are an equal number of starters, mains and desserts.
       How many of each are there ?

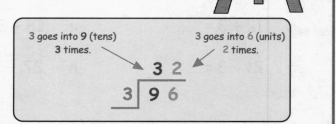

Be able to divide a 2 digit number by 3 with no remainder.

When **dividing** into **larger numbers** you have to do so in 2 steps.

Example :- What is **9** 6 ÷ **3** ?

3 goes into 9 (tens) 3 times.   3 goes into 6 (units) 2 times.

```
    3 2
3 | 9 6
```

Exercise 4

1. **Copy** and **complete** :-

   a 3 | 39   b 3 | 66   c 3 | 30   d 3 | 69

   e 3 | 33   f 3 | 36   g 3 | 60   h 3 | 90

   i 3 | 63   j 3 | 93   k 3 | 96   l 3 | 99.

2. **36** strawberries were spread equally amongst **3** ice-creams.
   How many strawberries were in each bowl of ice-cream ?

3.

   3 pots had a total of **99** gold coins.
   Each pot had the same number of coins.
   How many were in each pot ?

4. A potato grower has only **45** Jersey potatoes left.
   She puts them equally into **3** bags.
   How many are in each bag ?

5.

   Brian waters his plants **three** times each day.
   How many days has he been watering his plants,
   if up till now he has watered them **33** times ?

Dividing by 3 - Remainders

Be able to divide by 3 when there is a remainder.

3 boys were sharing out 8 chocolate coins.

The first boy got 2 coins.

The second boy got 2 coins.

The third boy got 2 coins.

This uses up 6 coins, so there are 2 coins left over.

We say that 8 (chocolate coins) shared by 3 gives 2 each, remainder 2.

remainder 2

8 ÷ 3 = 2 remainder 2   or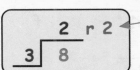

Your teacher will explain this to you :-

Example 1 :- What is 9 5 ÷ 3 ?

3 goes into 9 (tens) 3 times.

3 goes into 5 (units) 1 times remainder 2.

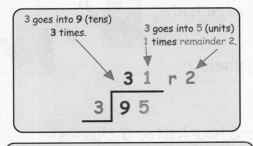

9 5 ÷ 3 = 3 1 remainder 2

Example 2 :- What is 7 2 ÷ 3 ?

3 goes into 7 (tens) 2 times remainder 1.

The 2 becomes 12.

3 goes into 12 (units) 4 times.

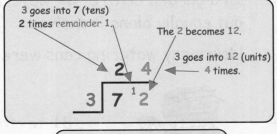

7 2 ÷ 3 = 2 4

Example 3 :- What is 4 6 ÷ 3 ?

3 goes into 4 (tens) 1 times remainder 1.

The 6 becomes 16.

3 goes into 16 (units) 5 times remainder 1.

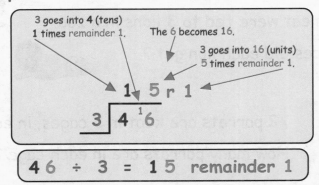

4 6 ÷ 3 = 1 5 remainder 1

1. Copy and complete :-

   a   13 ÷ 3 = ...   b   16 ÷ 3 = ...   c   20 ÷ 3 = ...   d   10 ÷ 3 = ...

   e   7 ÷ 3 = ...   f   14 ÷ 3 = ...   g   19 ÷ 3 = ...   h   26 ÷ 3 = ...

   i   22 ÷ 3 = ...   j   25 ÷ 3 = ...   k   29 ÷ 3 = ...   l   11 ÷ 3 = ...

2. Copy and complete these divisions :-

   a   3)27   b   3)36   c   3)42   d   3)48

   e   3)51   f   3)57   g   3)72   h   3)78

   i   3)84   j   3)87   k   3)93   l   3)102.

   Set down as division sums and work them out to answer each question.

3. In a garden centre, 54 watering cans were laid out equally along 3 shelves.

   How many watering cans were on each shelf ?

4. 81 textbooks were bought for 3 classes.

   How many books did each class get ?

5. 18 pieces of meat were fed to 3 lions in a zoo.

   How many pieces did each lion get ?

6. 72 parrots are kept in 3 cages, in equal numbers.

   How many parrots are in each cage ?

7. Copy and complete :-

  a 3|32   b 3|34   c 3|61   d 3|35

  e 3|67   f 3|62   g 3|94   h 3|47

  i 3|73   j 3|83   k 3|88   l 3|92.

8. a 17 biscuits were shared equally among three dogs.

     How many did each dog get and how many were left over ?

  b  68 sardines were divided equally among 3 tins.

     How many sardines went in each tin
     and how many were left ?

  c Their grandpa gave Joyce, Paula and May 49 £1 coins
     to be shared equally among them.

     How many coins did each get and how many were left ?

  d  74 cabbage plants were split equally into
     3 rows in a garden.

     How many plants were in each row
     and how many were not in the rows ?

9. Copy and complete :-

  a 3|43   b 3|53   c 3|20   d 3|10

  e 3|17   f 3|29   g 3|46   h 3|74

  i 3|76   j 3|85   k 3|98   l 3|103.

Remember - set down the following as division sums and work them out.

10. 77 crayfish were placed in 3 baskets.

    Each basket had the same number of crayfish in it.

    How many was that and how many extra fish were there ?

11. 52 windows in an office block have to be washed.

    Bob, Bill and Ben decide to wash the same number of windows.

    What is the most they each can wash and how many would that leave unwashed ?

12.  13 children turned up for swimming lessons.

    They were split into 3 equal groups.

    How many were in each group and how many children were left out ?

13. Claire's mum bought 38 bags of crisps for a party.

    Everyone was given 3 bags and her mum was left with 2.

    How many people must there have been at the party ?

14.  A total of 86 fish were shared equally among 3 seals.

    How many fish did each seal get and how many were left over ?

15. Ted's wife made him 23 sandwiches to take with him on his fishing trip. He shared them equally amongst himself and his 2 friends.

    a   How many sandwiches did each receive ?

    The rest went to the seagulls.

    b   How many did the seagulls get to eat ?

1. Copy and complete :-

a 2)27   b 3)51   c 5)28   d 3)31

e 2)45   f 3)38   g 2)40   h 3)45

i 5)59   j 2)52   k 3)61   l 5)67

m 3)67   n 10)69   o 3)81   p 2)76.

2. The recipe says I need 40 ml of milk and the
    only measuring spoon I have holds 3 ml.

    How many full 3 ml spoonfuls will I have to use and how
    much more milk will there be in the final spoonful ?

3.    Jack buys 51 metres of rope to make skipping
       ropes for his gym class.

       If each rope has to be 2 metres long, how many can
       he make and what length of rope will not be used ?

4. Last night, it took Cheryl's brother 5 times as
    long as her to do his homework.

    It took him 45 minutes. How long did it take Cheryl ?

5.    Joe is out to spend his £79 birthday money.

       After buying the top 2 computer games
       (both at the same price) he still has £1 to spend.

       a   How much was each game ?

       b   He buys 3 lollies with the £1
            and still has 1p left.

            How much was each lolly ?

1. Copy and work out :-

   a $2\overline{)92}$ b $3\overline{)69}$ c $10\overline{)77}$ d $5\overline{)95}$

   e $3\overline{)200}$ f $5\overline{)295}$ g $2\overline{)308}$ h $3\overline{)152}$.

2. Find :-

   a $106 \div 2$ b $117 \div 3$ c $96 \div 4$ d $410 \div 5$

   e $189 \div 4$ f $319 \div 2$ g $334 \div 5$ h $294 \div 3$.

3. Mrs Amos buys 20 toy cars to be shared among her 3 boys.

   How many will each boy get and how many will be left over ?

4.  The canoes at the boating pond hold 3 people.

   What is the least number of canoes that will be needed to carry 40 people and how many canoes will have less than 3 in them ?

5. It cost John and his 2 brothers £981 altogether to go on holiday to Spain.

   How much did they each have to pay ?

6. A cider manufacturer ordered 840 apples.

   They were delivered in 5 vans, each van carrying 3 large baskets of apples.

   How many apples were in each basket ?

Time - Digital and Analogue Revision

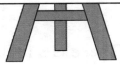

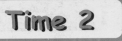
Be able to tell the time using analogue and digital clocks.

 Exercise 1

1. How many minutes are there in one hour ?

2. Write down the time on each digital clock in words :-

   a 7:30   b 2:15   c 3:45

   d 8:05   e 9:55   f 3:00

3. Write down the time on each clock in 2 ways :-
   (*e.g. quarter to ten in the morning* and *9:45 am*)

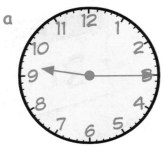

just started school

evening news

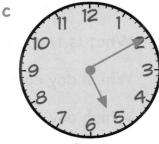

dinner

breakfast

lunch

asleep

4. Write out each of these times fully :-
   (Use " *in the morning* ", "*in the afternoon* ", or "*at night*").

   a 8:25 pm   b 7:15 am   c 10:10 pm

   d 6:03 am   e 4:17 pm   f 12:10 pm.

The Calendar

Remember :-

There are **7** days in a **week**.

There are **12** months in a **year**.

There are **365** days in a **year**. *(366 in a leap year.)*

There is a little rhyme that helps you remember how many days there are in each month. There are other ways of remembering them also.

30 days has September, April,
June and November.
All the rest have 31, except
February which has 28 days clear
and 29 in each leap year.

Exercise 2

1. a What is the 1st month of the year ?

    b What is the **last** month of the year ?

    c Which day comes 2 days **after** Thursday ?

    d Which day comes 3 days before **before** Monday ?

    e Which month comes 3 months **after** July ?

    f Which month comes 4 months **before** May ?

2. How many days are there in the month of :-

    a January   b February   c April   d June

    e August   f October   g November   h December ?

3. What is the :-

    a 6th month   b 3rd month   c 10th month   d 8th month ?

The date, 3rd of January 2012 can be written using 6 digits.

3rd Jan 2012

2012	JANUARY	2012
SUN	MON	TUES	WED	THU	FRI	SAT
1	2	③	4	5	6	7
8	9	10	11	12	13	14
15	16	17	18	19	20	21
22	23	24	25	26	27	28
29	30	31	*	*	*	*

3rd January, 2012 = 03 : 01 : 12 or 03/01/12

↑ day ↑ month ↑ year

4. Write each of these dates using 6 digits as above :–

a 24th March 2015   b 20th January 2014   c 23rd June 2011

d 19th September 2018   e 8th July 2010   f 4th April 2020

g 11th December 2009   h 2nd February 2017   i 5th May 2017.

5. Write each of these dates in words :–

a 13/02/12   b 02/04/15   c 10/10/10

d 22/03/04   e 09:09:09   f 06:07:16

g 08:01:20   h 31:04:15   i 30/02/10.

6. What is wrong with Questions 5 h and 5 i ?

7. Look at the month of April 2014.

a How many Wednesdays were in April 2014 ?

b Ellie had her birthday on 03/04/14.
   On what day was her birthday ?

c Teri has her birthday exactly
   3 weeks after Ellie.
   Teri had her birthday on what date ?

d Chad's birthday is 3 days before Ellie's.
   What date was Chad's birthday ?

April 2014

Su	Mo	Tu	We	Th	Fr	Sa
		1	2	3	4	5
6	7	8	9	10	11	12
13	14	15	16	17	18	19
20	21	22	23	24	25	26
27	28	29	30			

8. Look at the two calendar months shown.

May 2015

Mo	Tu	We	Th	Fr	Sa	Su
				1	2	3
4	5	6	7	8	9	10
11	12	13	14	15	16	17
18	19	20	21	22	23	24
25	26	27	28	29	30	31

   a   How many Saturdays are there **altogether** in May **and** June 2015 ?

   b   My birthday is on May 14th.

           My sister has her birthday exactly 3 weeks later.

           What date is my sister's birthday ?

June 2015

Mo	Tu	We	Th	Fr	Sa	Su
1	2	3	4	5	6	7
8	9	10	11	12	13	14
15	16	17	18	19	20	21
22	23	24	25	26	27	28
29	30					

9. What is the day and the date :-

   a   one day before 1st of May 2015

   b   two days after 30th of June 2015

   c   a week after 24th June 2015

   d   a week before 12th June 2015

   e   2 weeks after 8th May 2015

   f   1 week after 25th May 2015 ?

10. How many days are there between (*do not include the dates*) :-

   a   March the 4th to 15th b   April 11th to 29th

   c   02/02/14 to 23/02/14   d   30/05/13 to 02/06/13

   e   the 20th of June to 3rd of August ?

11. a   Today is June 5th. My birthday is on June 15th
           How many days to go to my birthday ? (*Don't include the 5th*).

   b   Today is April 28th. I am going to a show on May 3rd.
           How many days till I go to the show ? (*Don't include the 28th*).

12. Find out how often **leap years** occur. When are the next 2 leap years ?

Units of Time

There are 60 seconds in one minute.

There are 60 minutes in one hour.

There are 24 hours in one day.

Be able to decide what unit of time to use to measure an activity.

Exercise 3

1. Would you measure each of these in seconds, minutes, hours, or days ?

   a   walking to school
   b   walking across the classroom
   c   walking all round Wales
   d   doing a 500 piece jigsaw
   e   writing your name
   f   a marathon run (26 miles)
   g   boiling an egg
   h   watching two DVD films
   i   swimming one length
   j   growing a plant ?

2. List two or three activities that would take :-

   a   seconds
   b   minutes
   c   hours
   d   days.

3. How many seconds are there in :-

   a   2 minutes
   b   3 minutes
   c   5 mins
   d   8 mins
   e   half a minute
   f   4 mins
   g   10 mins
   h   20 mins ?

4. How many minutes are there in :-

   a   2 hours
   b   4 hours
   c   5 hours
   d   10 hours
   e   3 hours
   f   half an hour
   g   one hour
   h   quarter of an hour ?

5. **Copy** the diagram and **match** which time would go with which activity :-

6. Copy the diagram and match which time would go with which activity :-

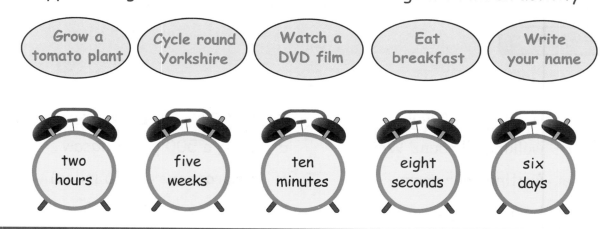

7. Use an encyclopaedia or the internet to find information about the fastest man or woman to run :-

    a   100 metres   b   one mile   c   a marathon.

8. Make a poster for one of the following or pick a topic yourself.
    (*Use an encyclopaedia or the internet to find information*) :-

    a   How fast different types of penguins can swim
        compared to how fast a human can swim.

    b   Different speeds of aircraft
        (small plane, jumbo jet, fighter jet, ...).

    c   Different speeds of boats
        (rowing boat, speed boat, cruise liner, ...).

    d   The slowest moving animals.

Be able to time events using a watch or stopwatch.

You can time how long something takes by using a **watch**, (*preferably with a second hand*) or a **stop watch**.

Exercise 4 *(You need a watch with a second hand, or a stopwatch).*

1. **Estimate** how long it would take you (*to the nearest minute*) to complete each of the following :–

   a   walk from one classroom wall to the opposite wall

   b   walk from one end of the corridor to the other

   c   walk all the way round the outside of the school

   d   jog all the way round the outside of the school

   e   add up all the numbers from 1 to 20 (*correctly*)

   f   write out the alphabet *backwards* (*correctly*)

   g   solve a puzzle or tangram given to you by your teacher

   h   get up from bed and get ready for school yourself

   i   make and eat your own breakfast

   j   walk (or be driven) home from school.

2. Now time some or all of the activities in Question 1, using a watch or stopwatch. Answer in minutes and seconds.

3. Stopwatches can have "read-outs" that look like this.

   a   Find out the meaning of this read out (*especially the 7*).

   b   Investigate what sports or activities use this kind of read out.

   c   Why do you think they have to use this kind of read-out ?

Revisit - Review - Revise

1. a   What is the day just before Wednesday ?

    b   Which day comes 3 days after Friday ?

    c   Which month comes 3 months after June ?

    d   Which month comes 4 months before January ?

2.   How many days are there in :-

    a   January   b   June   c   a leap year ?

3.   What is the :-

    a   6th month   b   3rd month   c   10th month ?

4.   Write each of these dates using only words :-

    a   12 / 05 / 15   b   01 / 01 / 20   c   07 / 06 / 05.

5.   Write each of the following using only numbers :-

    a   fifth of August two thousand and sixteen

    b   twentieth of October two thousand and nineteen.

6.   Shown is the calendar tab for July 2015.

    a   How many Fridays are in July 2015 ?

    b   What day is the 1st of August 2015 ?

    c   What day is the 29th of June 2015 ?

July 2015						
Mo	Tu	We	Th	Fr	Sa	Su
		1	2	3	4	5
6	7	8	9	10	11	12
13	14	15	16	17	18	19
20	21	22	23	24	25	26
27	28	29	30	31		

7.   List two activities that you might time yourself in :-

    a   seconds   b   minutes   c   hours.

Dividing by 4 (No Remainder)

Be able to divide a 2 digit number by 4 (no remainder).

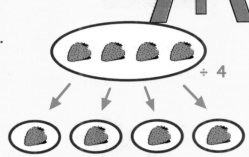

Dividing by 4 is the same as sharing equally among four.

Sam has 4 strawberries.

He shares them with Aaron, Joan and Pete.
All four each get 1 strawberry.

We say that   4 divided by 4 = 1.

or $4 \div 4 = 1$

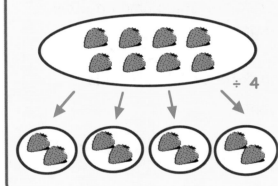

Julie has 8 strawberries.
She shares them with Pat, Nan and Ian.
They each get 2 strawberries.

We say that   8 divided by 4 = 2.

or $8 \div 4 = 2$

Exercise 1

1. Write out your 4 times table and use it to help in this exercise.

2. Copy and complete :-

   a $12 \div 4 = ...$ b $8 \div 4 = ...$ c $16 \div 4 = ...$

   d $24 \div 4 = ...$ e $20 \div 4 = ...$ f $28 \div 4 = ...$

   g $36 \div 4 = ...$ h $32 \div 4 = ...$ i $40 \div 4 = ...$

3. Find the missing numbers here :-

   a   ( ) $\div 4 = 5$ b   ( ) $\div 4 = 10$ c   ( ) $\div 4 = 7$

   d   ( ) $\div 4 = 6$ e   ( ) $\div 4 = 9$ f   ( ) $\div 4 = 8.$

4. Try these questions **mentally**.

a   **4** children share out **32** flowers equally.

How many do they get each ?

b    There are **40** pencils in **4** full boxes.

How many pencils are in each box ?

c   A bunch of bananas contains **4** bananas.

How many bunches would **28** bananas make ?

d    Frank bought **16** biscuits for his **four** dogs.

If he gave each dog the same amount, how many would each get ?

e   When **4** girls went golfing they lost a total of **12** golf balls.

They each lost the same number of balls.

How many was that ?

f   It cost **£36** for **four** child tickets to the final of the tennis competition.

What was the price of a ticket ?

Remember :-

$48 \div 4 = ...$
can be written as :-

```
   1 2
4 | 4 8
```

How many 4's are in the 4 ? answer **1**
How many 4's are in the 8 ? answer **2**

---

5. **Copy** and **complete** these :-

a $4\overline{)40}$

b $4\overline{)48}$

c $4\overline{)44}$

d $4\overline{)80}$

e $4\overline{)84}$

f $4\overline{)88}$.

Set down each question as a division sum and work it out.

6. a It took Tam **84** seconds to eat **4** burgers.

   How long would it have taken him to eat one ?

b  Kim bought **4** identical joysticks for a total of **£48**.

   How much did they each cost ?

c A box of **88** fries was shared among **4** children.

   How many did each of them get ?

d  A pineapple is quartered by cutting it into **4** slices.

   If I have **40** slices, how many whole pineapples
   must I have had to cut up ?

| Dividing by 4 - Remainders |

> Be able to
> divide a 2 digit
> number by 4
> (with a remainder).

Example 1 :-

$45 \div 4 = ...$
can be written as :-

$$\begin{array}{r} 1\ 1\ \text{r}\ 1 \\ 4\overline{)\ 4\ 5} \end{array}$$

How many 4's are in **4** ? ans **1**

How many 4's are in **5** ? ans **1 r 1**

| **1 1 r 1** |

Example 2 :-

remainder 1
is carried

$52 \div 4 = ...$
can be written as :-

$$\begin{array}{r} 1\ 3 \\ 4\overline{)\ 5\ {}^1 2} \end{array}$$

How many 4's are in **5** ? ans **1 r 1**

How many 4's are in **12** ? ans **3**

| **1 3** |

remainder 2 is carried
and still another
remainder appears

Example 3 :-

$67 \div 4 = ...$
can be written as :-

$$\begin{array}{r} 1\ 6\ \text{r}\ 3 \\ 4\overline{)\ 6\ {}^2 7} \end{array}$$

How many 4's are in **6** ? ans **1 r 2**

How many 4's are in **27** ? ans **6 r 3**

| **1 6 r 3** |

1. Copy and complete :-

   a   13 ÷ 4 = ...   b   11 ÷ 4 = ...   c   14 ÷ 4 = ...

   d   23 ÷ 4 = ...   e   9 ÷ 4 = ...   f   7 ÷ 4 = ...

   g   18 ÷ 4 = ...   h   15 ÷ 4 = ...   i   19 ÷ 4 = ...

2. Set down and work out :-

   a $4\overline{)42}$ b $4\overline{)43}$ c $4\overline{)46}$ d $4\overline{)49}$

   e $4\overline{)81}$ f $4\overline{)82}$ g $4\overline{)85}$ h $4\overline{)87}$.

Remember :- set down the following as division sums and work them out.

3. a   **17** slices of lasagne were divided among **4** diners.

      How many slices did each get and how many were left over ?

   b      **41** receipts were placed equally into **4** folders.

      How many receipts went in each folder and how many were left out ?

   c   **4** envelopes were used to keep **89** stamps in.

      Each envelope had the same number of stamps.

      How many were in each envelope and how many were left out ?

   d      Playing in the garden, Joe and his **3** pals divided **83** water balloons between them and gave the rest to Joe's sister Mandy.

      How many water balloons did Mandy get ?

   e   I'm thinking of a big number. When I divide it by **4**, I get the answer **15**, remainder **3**.

      What number am I thinking about ?

4. Copy and complete :-

a $4\overline{)28}$ b $4\overline{)32}$ c $4\overline{)40}$ d $4\overline{)52}$

e $4\overline{)56}$ f $4\overline{)68}$ g $4\overline{)64}$ h $4\overline{)60}$

i $4\overline{)72}$ j $4\overline{)76}$ k $4\overline{)92}$ l $4\overline{)96}$.

5. a My plants have to be fed every 4 days.

   If I were to go on holiday for 36 days, how many
   times would my neighbour have to feed the plants ?

b  48 tyres have to be put on to 4 identical trucks.

   How many tyres will be on each truck ?

c Four girls collected a total of £84 during a poppy appeal.

   If they each collected the same amount, how much was that ?

d   Pizza slices are to be put into boxes, 4 to a box.

   How many boxes will be needed for 76 slices ?

e The total cost for 4 pre-theatre dinners came to £68.

   What was the cost for one dinner ?

6. Copy and complete :-

a $4\overline{)62}$ b $4\overline{)55}$ c $4\overline{)73}$ d $4\overline{)58}$

e $4\overline{)71}$ f $4\overline{)93}$ g $4\overline{)74}$ h $4\overline{)95}$

i $4\overline{)99}$ j $4\overline{)26}$ k $4\overline{)39}$ l $4\overline{)102}$.

7. a   Gleamo Cleaning Company bought 63 scrubbing brushes
        and divided them among its 4 employees.

    How many brushes did they each get and how many were left ?

    b      The council made 70 roundabout signs to be
            put up in 4 of its new towns, each town getting
            the same number.

            How many signs did each town get and how many
            signs were not used ?

    c   65 formula one racing cars lined up in 4's on the starting grid.

    How many rows of four were there
    and how many cars were on the back row ?

    d      97 metre strips of guttering were used
            in building 4 identical houses on a new estate.

            How many metres were used on each house
            and how many metres were left over ?

    e   39 golfers turned up to play in a foursome competition.

    How many groups of 4 were formed and how
    many players were needed to make up another group ?

    f      There are 54 headache tablets in a packet.

            If Gemma takes 2 tablets twice per day, how
            many days will the packet last - but what will
            Gemma have to do on the last day ?

8. Copy these divisions and work them out :-

    a   4 $\overline{\smash{)}\,27}$ b   4 $\overline{\smash{)}\,29}$ c   4 $\overline{\smash{)}\,34}$ d   4 $\overline{\smash{)}\,37}$

    e   4 $\overline{\smash{)}\,44}$ f   4 $\overline{\smash{)}\,51}$ g   4 $\overline{\smash{)}\,57}$ h   4 $\overline{\smash{)}\,61}$

    i   4 $\overline{\smash{)}\,66}$ j   4 $\overline{\smash{)}\,72}$ k   4 $\overline{\smash{)}\,79}$ l   4 $\overline{\smash{)}\,86}$.

Dividing into 3 digits

> Be able to divide any 3 digit number by 2, 3, 4, 5 or 10.

Example 1 :- 145 ÷ 2

```
    7 2 r 1
2 ⌐1 4 5
```

Example 2 :- 224 ÷ 3

```
    7 4 r 2
3 ⌐2 2 2¹4
```

Example 3 :- 251 ÷ 4

```
    6 2 r 3
4 ⌐2 5 ¹1
```

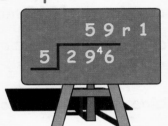

Example 4 :- 296 ÷ 5

```
    5 9 r 1
5 ⌐2 9 ⁴6
```

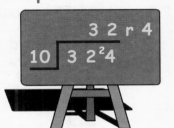

Example 5 :- 324 ÷ 10

```
     3 2 r 4
10 ⌐3 2 ²4
```

Exercise 3

1. Copy and complete :-

   a 2)143   b 3)225   c 4)252   d 5)297

   e 3)174   f 4)268   g 5)285   h 2)195

   i 4)149   j 5)243   k 10)173   l 3)179 .

2. Set these down like Question 1 and work them out :-

   a 105 ÷ 2 = ...   b 206 ÷ 3 = ...   c 262 ÷ 4 = ...

   d 300 ÷ 5 = ...   e 290 ÷ 10 = ...   f 121 ÷ 4 = ...

   g 212 ÷ 5 = ...   h 113 ÷ 2 = ...   i 200 ÷ 3 = ...

   j 281 ÷ 4 = ...   k 239 ÷ 5 = ...   l 300 ÷ 4 = ...

   m 170 ÷ 10 = ...   n 218 ÷ 3 = ...   o 199 ÷ 5 = ...

Set down these questions as division sums and work them out.

3. Mr Davis bought a £258 sofa and paid it up over 3 months.

   How much was each monthly payment ?

4.  The total number of runs scored in 2 cricket matches was 178.

   If the same number of runs was scored in each match, how many was that ?

5. Terry and June took 5 hours to travel 295 miles.

   At the same speed, how far would they have gone in 1 hour ?

6. Geraldine is paid £152 for working 4 hours.

   What does she get paid for 1 hour's work ?

7. 165 bags of gritting salt was loaded equally onto 2 lorries.

   How many were in each lorry and how many were left out ?

8. A 260 ml carton of orange juice was poured into 4 identical glasses.

   How many ml did each glass hold ?

9.  A supermarket took in £350 from the sale of £10 boxes of dark chocolates.

   How many boxes did they sell ?

10. A shopkeeper has put 5 apples into each of 24 bags.

    Charlie buys all the apples.

    He gives 4 apples to each of his classmates.

    How many classmates does Charlie have ?

Mixed Exercise

Exercise 4

Be able to add, subtract, multiply or divide by 2, 3, 4, 5 or 10.

1. Copy and work out :-

a
```
  23
+  9
```

b
```
  56
-  8
```

c
```
  57
×  2
```

d
```
   23
× 10
```

e
```
  286
-  51
```

f
```
  86
+ 79
```

g $2\overline{)18}$

h $5\overline{)65}$

i
```
  513
-  84
```

j
```
  78
×  3
```

k
```
   45
+ 397
```

l
```
  289
+  67
```

m
```
  98
×  4
```

n $3\overline{)102}$

o
```
  812
- 594
```

p
```
  900
- 234
```

q
```
  632
+ 189
```

r
```
  82
×  5
```

s $4\overline{)276}$

t $2\overline{)175}$.

2. Set down and find :-

a $7 + 45$

b $63 - 18$

c 75×2

d 46×3

e $275 \div 5$

f $47 + 73$

g $316 - 25$

h $29 \div 2$

i 94×3

j $56 \div 4$

k 87×5

l $200 - 91$

m $926 - 345$

n $628 + 295$

o 84×10

p $132 \div 5$

q $237 \div 3$

r $210 \div 10$

s 4×72

t 75×5

u $3 \times 4 \times 5 \times 4$

v $4 \times 70 \div 10$

w $80 \div 5 - 6$

x $19 - 20$.
careful

3. Most new cars nowadays don't come with a spare wheel, so you have to pay extra if you want one ....

   £68 for a metal wheel and another £73 for a tyre.

   How much does that come to ?

4.  A tree has 94 leaves on it.

   On each leaf there are 3 ladybirds.

   How many ladybirds in total are there on the tree ?

5. To fly with Timothy Crook to Gran Canaria costs £289 return.

   Flying with Jet3 costs £412 return.

   By how much is Timothy Crook cheaper ?

6.  A mechanic puts 4 litres of oil into all the cars he services.

   If he serviced 38 cars last month, how much oil did he use ?

7. A janitor lays out chairs in rows of five.

   If he puts out 80 chairs, how many rows will there be ?

8. There are 29 lollies in this jar.

   There are 4 jars of them on display in each of 2 shops.

   How many lollies in total are up for sale ?

9.  Moira's fees for gym membership are £285.

   She is also in a bowling club, costing £198.

   How much does she pay in total ?

Revisit - Review - Revise

1. **Copy** and **work out** :-

   a $4\overline{)44}$ b $4\overline{)72}$ c $4\overline{)93}$ d $4\overline{)86}$

   e $4\overline{)208}$ f $4\overline{)112}$ g $4\overline{)171}$ h $4\overline{)195}$.

2. **Find** :-

   a $119 \div 2$ b $217 \div 3$ c $152 \div 4$ d $257 \div 5$

   e $207 \div 10$ f $200 \div 2$ g $219 \div 4$ h $126 \div 4$.

3. Goldfish are to be placed in bowls, maximum **4** to a bowl.

   A pet shop has **215** goldfish.

   How many bowls are needed ?

4. Mel bought a **£388** motorbike and paid it up over **4** months.

   How much did she pay each month ?

5. A department store bought in **258** pairs of jeans.

   There was an equal number of large, medium and small sizes.

   How many medium sized jeans were bought in ?

6. Jane and Sheila shared a **£280** win at the bingo.

   Jane split her winnings evenly between herself, her husband and 2 daughters.

   How much did Jane's husband get ?

Chapter 14

Reading from Tables and Charts Revision

Looking back at reading tables and charts from year 2.

Exercise 1

1. A DIY store has posted a list of adult classes for the day.

Starting Times	Activity	Where ?
11.00	Joinery	Area 12
12.30	Gardening	Nursery
2.00	Plumbing	Area 26
3.15	Decorating	Paint Desk

    a   What time does the plumbing start ?

    b   Where does the gardening class take place ?

    c   Jason is about to attempt to put on wallpaper in his living room.

    Which class should he go to ? When is it - and where ?

2. The table shows the prices of short stay hotel breaks from Leeds.

    a   How much would it cost to go to Cardiff for 3 nights ?

	2 nights	3 nights	4 nights	1 week
Cardiff	£80	£100	£120	£180
London	£160	£180	£210	£290
Paris	£340	£370	£400	£520

    b   How much would it cost to go to London for a week ?

    c   How much for 4 nights in Paris ? In which country is Paris ?

    d   Alice spent £180 on a short stay holiday.

    Which one of 2 places could she have gone to and for how long ?

3. This pictograph shows the number of trees that were planted in a school garden.

Key: 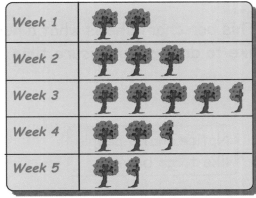 stands for 10 trees.

a How many trees were planted in week 1 ? (*Not 2*).

b How many in week 3 ?

c How many in week 4 and week 5 altogether ?

4. A group of pupils were asked to name their favourite sport.

The results are shown in the block diagram.

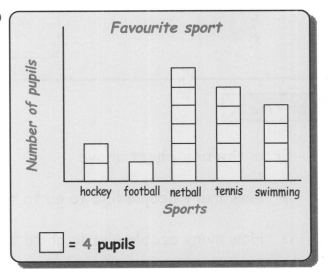

a How many pupils chose football ?

b How many chose hockey ?

c How many chose tennis ?

d How many chose swimming ?

e How many more preferred netball to swimming ?

f How many less chose football compared to tennis ?

g The survey was done at either an all boys' or an all girls' school.

Which one do you think it was ? - and say why.

Reading from a Bar Chart

Be able to interpret information from a bar chart.

This bar chart shows what a number of people like to do in their leisure time.

Notice that 3 people like to go bowling.

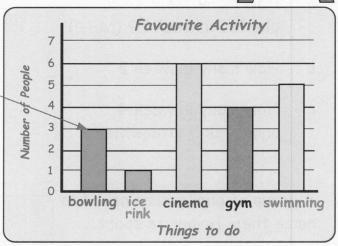

Favourite Activity

Number of People (vertical axis: 0, 1, 2, 3, 4, 5, 6, 7)

Things to do: bowling, ice rink, cinema, gym, swimming

Exercise 2

1. From the **bar chart** above :-

   a   How many people like to go to the ice rink ?

   b   How many people like to go to the cinema ?

   c   How many people like to go swimming ?

   d   How many people like to go to the gym ?

   e   What is the **most** popular thing to do ?

   f   Where is the **least** popular place to go ?

   g   How many **more** people chose the cinema than the ice rink ?

   h   How many people were asked in **total** ?

   i   How many people did **not** choose to go to the cinema ?

2. The bar chart shows the favourite computer games of a Year 3 class.

    a   How many pupils chose Blue Rain ?

    b   How many chose Red Alert ?

    c   How many chose Duty Calls ?

    d   How many chose Cowboy Joe ?

    e   What was the **most** popular game ?

    f   How many pupils **altogether** were asked about their computer games ?

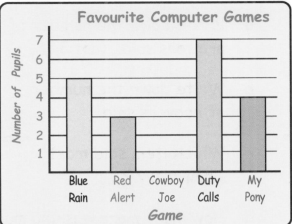

3. This bar chart shows the number of boxes of crisps eaten at the school disco.

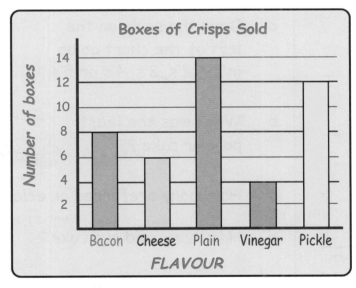

    a   How many boxes of **each** were eaten ?

    b   What was the **most** popular flavour of crisp ?

    c   What was the **least** popular flavour ?

    d   How many **more** boxes of **pickle** than **bacon** crisps were eaten ?

    e   How many **fewer** boxes of **vinegar** than **plain** crisps were eaten ?

    f   How many boxes of crisps were eaten **altogether** ?

4. The bar chart shows the number of items sold in an electrical store one Friday.

   a Write down the number of printers sold. (not 3 !)

   b Write down the number of hoovers sold.

   c Which item sold most - how many ?

   d How many more washing machines than hoovers were sold ?

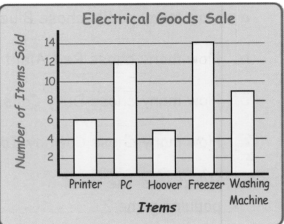

Electrical Goods Sale

Number of Items Sold: 14, 12, 10, 8, 6, 4, 2

Items: Printer, PC, Hoover, Freezer, Washing Machine

5. The bar chart here shows what kind of home baking elderly people prefer with a cup of tea.

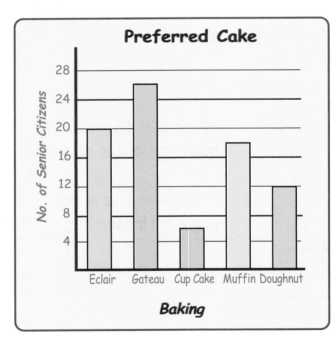

Preferred Cake

No. of Senior Citizens: 28, 24, 20, 16, 12, 8, 4

Baking: Eclair, Gateau, Cup Cake, Muffin, Doughnut

   a Does the scale on the left of the chart go up in 1's, 2's, 3's, 4's or 5's ?

   b What was the least popular cake ?

   c How many preferred an eclair ?

   d How many said cup cake ?

   e How many said doughnut ?

   f How many altogether said muffin or doughnut ?

   g How many more preferred gateau to eclair ?

6. Some people were asked what they would buy if they won a lot of money.

   Their answers are shown in a horizontal bar chart.

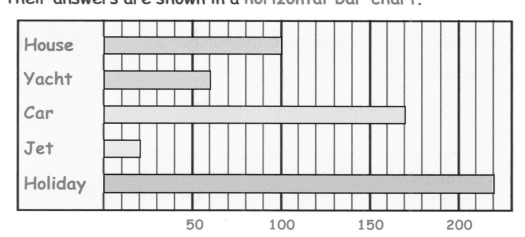

a   How many people would buy a house ?

b   How many would spend the money on a car ?

c   What was the most popular answer ? .... How many voted for that ?

d   How many more preferred their own yacht to a private jet ?

e   How many people were asked ?

7. Some children in Kent were asked which musical instrument they liked.

   Here are their answers :-

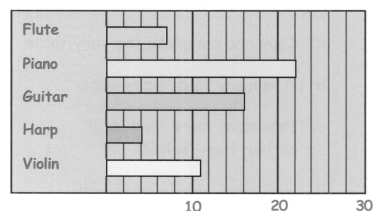

a   How many said harp ?
    (*not 2*).

b   How many said piano ?

c   How many said flute ?

d   How many more liked
    the guitar than the violin ?

e   How many children altogether were asked ?

Looking back at drawing charts and frequency tables from year 2.

Exercise 3

1. |||| are tally marks representing the number 5.

    Use tally marks to show :-

    a   9   b   13   c   24   d   36.

2. Use the given **key** to draw a **pictograph** showing the information which is in the table.

    Year 3 girls' favourite curry sauce.

Key: 🧍 stands for 2 girls

      🧍 = 1 girl

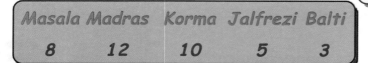

Masala	Madras	Korma	Jalfrezi	Balti
8	12	10	5	3

3. At a quiz night, one of the questions was to put a **word** before "................ **water**". The answers are shown in the table.

bottled	fizzy	still	fizzy	still
still	bottled	fizzy	still	still
fizzy	fizzy	still	fizzy	fizzy
salt	fizzy	bottled	fizzy	fizzy
bottled	fizzy	fizzy	fizzy	salt
fizzy	still	fizzy	bottled	fizzy

Word	Tally	Total
salt		
fizzy		

a   **Copy** and **complete** the tally table.

b   How many said "fizzy water" ?

c   How many **more** said "still" rather than "salt" ?

d   How many people answered the question ?

e   Draw a **block diagram** to show the information.

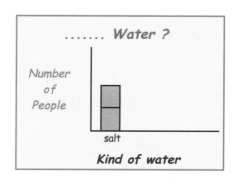

.... Water ?

Number of People

salt

Kind of water

Drawing Bar Charts

Drawing a Bar Chart

The table opposite shows what a number of people in a Fish and Chip Restaurant like to have with chips.

burger	-	16
sausage	-	2
cod	-	28
pizza	-	22
chicken	-	18

Be able to draw a bar chart.

This information can be displayed in a bar chart.

For a bar chart :-

- the scale should go up in equal amounts (4 here).

- the axes should be labelled clearly.

- it should have labels and a title.

- it should have equally spaced bars.

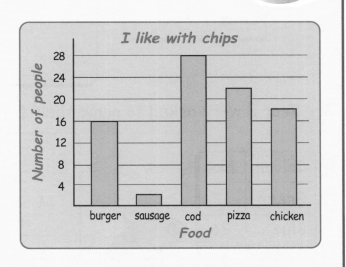

Exercise 4

Copy the bar chart in each question and use the information given in the table to complete it.

1. The hair colour of a group of children was recorded.

Colour	No.
Brown	14
Black	4
Blond	8
Red	2

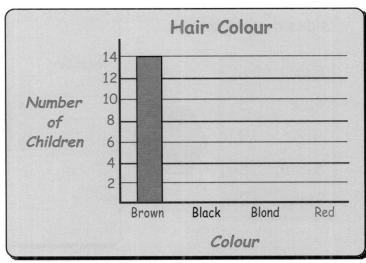

2. Some children were asked to name their favourite drink.

Drink	No.
Orange	8
Lemon	6
Apple	1
Cola	14
Lime	11

Favourite Drink

Number of Children

Orange Lemon Apple Cola Lime

Flavour

3. Year 3 were asked to name their favourite colours.

Colour	No.
Green	12
Blue	26
Red	20
Pink	4
Yellow	10

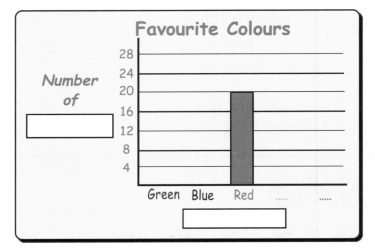

Favourite Colours

Number of

Green Blue Red ....

4. Children in a maths class were asked how many sides a **hexagon** has.

Four	6
Five	3
Six	9
Seven	8
Eight	2

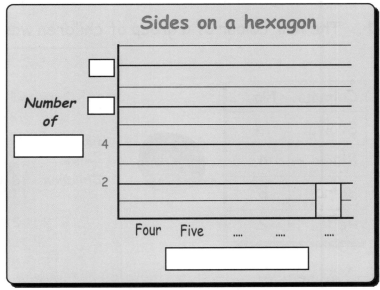

Sides on a hexagon

Number of

Four Five ....

5. Josie's family was asked how many teddy bears they owned when they were younger.

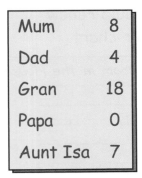

Mum	8
Dad	4
Gran	18
Papa	0
Aunt Isa	7

Family Teddy Bears

Number of

4
2

Family

Aunt Isa

6. 180 gardeners were asked what creatures they find in their gardens.

50	said	worms
30	said	ants
70	said	snails
25	said	beetles
5	said	spiders

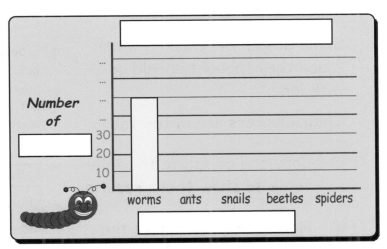

Number of

30
20
10

worms   ants   snails   beetles   spiders

7. Teachers at some schools were asked to name their favourite year group.

The results are shown in the table.

Draw a bar chart to show these.

The scale should go up in 2's.

Remember labels and headings.

Group	Number of Teachers
Year 1	6
Year 2	8
Year 3	12
Year 4	2
Year 5	9
Year 6	3

1. People were asked which room in the house they would renew if they had the money. Their answers are in the bar chart.

   a   Is the scale going up in 1's, 2's or 3's ?

   b   How many people said kitchen ?

   c   Which room was the least popular ?

   d   What is the **total** for bathroom and bedroom ?

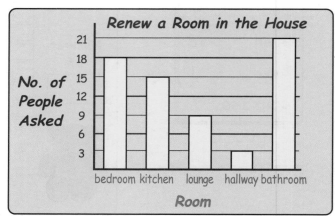

   e   How many **more** preferred kitchen to lounge ?

2. Some diners were asked which sauce they thought should go with lamb.

   Their answers are in the table.

Barbecue	Mint	Barbecue	Apple
Apple	Mint	Mint	Mint
Mushroom	Apple	Mint	Mint
Mint	Tomato	Barbecue	Apple
Tomato	Tomato	Apple	Mint
Mint	Mint	Tomato	Tomato

   a   Copy and complete the **tally table** to show these results.

   b   How many people gave the answer "tomato" ?

   c   How many people were asked ?

   d   How many people gave what is thought to be the "correct" answer ?

   e   Draw a **bar chart** from the table. (Remember the scale; title; headings; labels and bars).

Sauce	Tally	Total
Barbecue		
Apple		
Mint		
Mushroom		
Tomato		

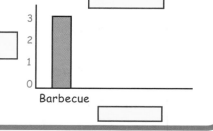

Chapter 15

Dividing by 8 (No Remainder)

Be able to divide a number by 8 (no remainder).

Remember your 8 times table ?

1 x 8 = 8	2 x 8 = 16	3 x 8 = 24	4 x 8 = 32	5 x 8 = 40	6 x 8 = 48
7 x 8 = 56	8 x 8 = 64	9 x 8 = 72	10 x 8 = 80	11 x 8 = 88	12 x 8 = 96

Example 1 :-

40 ÷ 8

40 ÷ 8 = 5
from knowing 8 x table.

Example 2 :-

96 ÷ 8

Example 3 :-

256 ÷ 8

Exercise 1

1. Copy each of these and complete :-

   a 8 ÷ 8 = ...

   b 32 ÷ 8 = ...

   c 16 ÷ 8 = ...

   d 56 ÷ 8 = ...

   e 24 ÷ 8 = ...

   f 40 ÷ 8 = ...

2. Find the missing numbers :-

   a ◯ ÷ 8 = 8

   b ◯ ÷ 8 = 2

   c ◯ ÷ 8 = 4

   d ◯ ÷ 8 = 7

   e ◯ ÷ 8 = 11

   f ◯ ÷ 8 = 12.

3. Copy and complete :-

   a 8 ⟌ 48

   b 8 ⟌ 88

   c 8 ⟌ 96

   d 8 ⟌ 104

   e 8 ⟌ 136

   f 8 ⟌ 240

   g 8 ⟌ 288

   h 8 ⟌ 144

   i 8 ⟌ 224

   j 8 ⟌ 128

   k 8 ⟌ 304

   l 8 ⟌ 248 .

4. Set these down like Question 3 and find the answers :-

   a $72 \div 8 = ...$ b $112 \div 8 = ...$ c $120 \div 8 = ...$

   d $152 \div 8 = ...$ e $296 \div 8 = ...$ f $400 \div 8 = ...$

5. Try these questions mentally :-

   a Zak's dad can remain underwater for 48 seconds.

      This is 8 times longer than Zak.

      For how long can Zak stay underwater ?

   b   32 sheep were split equally into 8 pens.

      How many in each pen ?

   c Holfords sold 56 bicycles over a period of 8 hours.

      How many bicycles per hour is that ?

   d  A butcher was selling these hams for £8 each.

      He took in £72 for selling a few.

      How many did he actually sell ?

   e At a business meeting there are 64 salesmen
      spread equally around 8 tables.

      How many are sitting round each table ?

   f  Fiona works a 40 hour week.

      If she works 8 hours a day, how many days
      does she work per week ?

   g A ball of string is 96 metres long.

      It is cut into 8 equal pieces to attach to 8 kites.

      What is the length of each piece of string ?

Set down these questions as division sums and work them out.

6. A rowing competition requires teams of 8 in each boat.

   How many teams can be made from 104 people ?

7.  Jessie bought 8 cushions from Debnim Stores for a total price of £136.

   What was the price of each cushion ?

8. Car vacuums are on sale at £8 each.

   A garage chain buys £200 worth.

   How many did they buy ?

9.  A company buys 112 pairs of trousers and gives them to a seamstress for alterations.

   If she alters 8 pairs an hour, how many hours will the whole job take ?

10. Kate has been saving £8 per week.

    How many weeks has she been saving if she now has £264 altogether ?

11.  8 people pay £808 in total for a city break.

    How much did each of them have to pay ?

12. The 168 people queuing in an airport departure lounge are placed into 8 equal rows to speed up checking in.

    How many are in each row ?

13. A paper clip is made from 8 cm of wire.

    How many can be made from 216 cm of wire ?

Dividing by 8 - Remainders

Be able to divide a number by 8 (with a remainder).

Example 1 :-

$89 \div 8 = ...$

can be written as :-

$$8 \overline{)\,8\;9\,}$$ $1\;1\; r\; 1$

How many 8's are in 8 ? ans **1**

How many 8's are in 9 ? ans **1 r 1**

Example 2 :-

$96 \div 8 = ...$

can be written as :-

$$8 \overline{)\,9\,{}^{1}6\,}$$ $1\; 2$

remainder 1 is carried

How many 8's are in 9 ? ans **1 r 1**

How many 8's are in 16 ? ans **2**

Example 3 :-

$283 \div 8 = ...$

can be written as :-

remainder 2 is carried

remainder 4 is carried and still another remainder appears

$$8 \overline{)\,2\,{}^{2}8\,{}^{4}3\,}$$ $0\; 3\; 5\; r\; 3$

How many 8's are in 2 ? ans **0 r 2**

How many 8's are in 28 ? ans **3 r 4**

How many 8's are in 43 ? ans **5 r 3**

Exercise 2

1. Copy and complete :-

    a $11 \div 8 = ...$ b $34 \div 8 = ...$ c $44 \div 8 = ...$

    d $52 \div 8 = ...$ e $55 \div 8 = ...$ f $62 \div 8 = ...$

    g $65 \div 8 = ...$ h $76 \div 8 = ...$ i $86 \div 8 = ...$

2. Set down and work out :-

    a $8\overline{)\,50\,}$ b $8\overline{)\,73\,}$ c $8\overline{)\,30\,}$ d $8\overline{)\,51\,}$

    e $8\overline{)\,85\,}$ f $8\overline{)\,71\,}$ g $8\overline{)\,81\,}$ h $8\overline{)\,75\,}$

    i $8\overline{)\,63\,}$ j $8\overline{)\,94\,}$ k $8\overline{)\,99\,}$ l $8\overline{)\,109\,}$.

3. Copy and complete :-

   a 8⟌172   b 8⟌225   c 8⟌293   d 8⟌130

   e 8⟌150   f 8⟌300   g 8⟌127   h 8⟌147 .

4. Set these down like Question 3 and find the answers :-

   a   51 ÷ 8 = ...   b   69 ÷ 8 = ...   c   104 ÷ 8 = ...

   d   268 ÷ 8 = ...   e   231 ÷ 8 = ...   f   286 ÷ 8 = ...

Set down these questions as division sums and work them out.

5.   Chocolate bites are on sale for 8p each.

      How many will I get for 90p and how much
      money will I have left ?

6.  A chemist shop has 205 bottles of talcum
      powder to be lined up along 8 shelves.

      How many bottles can go on each shelf and
      how many can not go on display yet ?

7. A zoo has ordered 230 bananas to feed its
    8 large monkeys over a period of time.

    How many will each monkey get and how
    many will be left for the staff to eat ?

8.  There are 259 frogs in a pond with 8 giant lilies in it.

      If they spread themselves evenly over the lilies, how
      many will be on each and how many will not get on ?

9. An ice cream shop ordered 292 kg of ice cream from the factory.

    If the ice cream comes in 8 kg tubs, how many tubs
    arrived and how many kg was in the extra small tub
    which made up the amount ordered ?

Mixed Exercise

Exercise 3

Be able to divide a number by 2, 3, 4, 5, 8 or 10.

1. Copy and complete :-

    a $2\overline{)7^14}$ ⟵ 3....

    b $3\overline{)57}$

    c $4\overline{)64}$

    d $5\overline{)65}$

    e $8\overline{)56}$

    f $10\overline{)98}$

    g $8\overline{)72}$

    h $4\overline{)57}$

    i $5\overline{)285}$

    j $3\overline{)258}$

    k $4\overline{)132}$

    l $2\overline{)199}$

    m $8\overline{)271}$

    n $4\overline{)158}$

    o $3\overline{)252}$

    p $8\overline{)284}$

    q $5\overline{)294}$

    r $3\overline{)290}$

    s $4\overline{)115}$

    t $8\overline{)328}$.

There are several ways of asking how we can represent :-

divide 94 by 4.

Here they are :-

94 divided by 4 $4\overline{)94}$ 4 into 94 $94 \div 4$ $\dfrac{94}{4}$

---

2. Write these in the form $3\overline{)72}$ and then work out the answer :-

    a $72 \div 3$

    b $4\overline{)136}$

    c $\dfrac{95}{5}$

    d 107 divided by 2

    e 8 into 143

    f $265 \div 5$

    g $\dfrac{280}{10}$

    h $2\overline{)158}$

    i 4 into 253

    j 303 divided by 3

    k $\dfrac{296}{8}$

    l $276 \div 4$.

3. Show all of your working for each of these problems :-

a There are 95 people in a tea room.

If each table can hold 5 people, how many tables are needed ?

b Nan can skate round the park in 3 minutes.

How many times can she go round in 42 minutes ?

c Mrs Moyer paid £196 for 2 identical tables.

What was the price of each table ?

d  Gran gave out 104 sweets to be shared amongst her 8 grandchildren.

How many sweets did they get each ?

e A farmer has 297 eggs to be put into packs with 10 eggs in each pack.

How many full packs can he make up ?

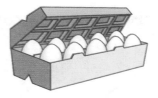

f I finished the 308 stages of my new computer game over 4 days, managing to finish the same number of stages each day.

How many stages was that each day ?

g An electrical store took in £388 selling 4 Kanon cameras.

How much was a Kanon camera ?

h Mrs Grace baked 172 scones for the church fete.

Half had fruit in them and half were plain scones.

How many fruit scones did she bake ?

1. Copy and work out :-

   a $8\overline{)72}$ b $8\overline{)96}$ c $8\overline{)152}$ d $8\overline{)264}$

   e $8\overline{)93}$ f $8\overline{)116}$ g $8\overline{)247}$ h $8\overline{)148}$.

2. Find :-

   a $73 \div 2$ b $215 \div 3$ c $123 \div 4$ d $245 \div 5$

   e $128 \div 8$ f $113 \div 10$ g $284 \div 8$ h $300 \div 8$.

3. 256 windows were used in building new cottages in a village.

   Each cottage had 8 windows.

   How many new cottages were built ?

4.  A jet can hold 288 passengers.

   There are 8 seats to a row.

   How many rows of seats does this jet have ?

5. The local Country & Western Band took in £304 for a Saturday evening show.

   Tickets for the show were priced £8 each.

   How many people had bought a ticket ?

6. 800 chocolate biscuits were put in boxes of 8.

   The boxes were then spread equally on to 5 shelves.

   How many boxes were on each shelf ?

Halves and Quarters Revision

Fractions 1

Understand how
to find a half
and a quarter
of something.

Exercise 1

1. Explain what you would do to find a half of something.

2. Find the following :- a $\frac{1}{2}$ of 10p b $\frac{1}{2}$ of 18 grams

   c $\frac{1}{2}$ of £28 d $\frac{1}{4}$ of 36 cm e $\frac{1}{4}$ of 80 m.

3. Talia has **26** dolls in her toy box.

   $\frac{1}{2}$ of them have a blue hair ribbon.

   How many dolls have a blue hair ribbon ?

4. Trace or draw this rectangle.

   a   Colour in any $\frac{1}{2}$ of the shape red.

   b   Now colour in any $\frac{1}{4}$ of it blue.

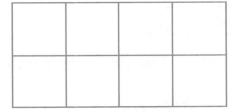

5. What fraction of these shapes has been coloured ?

   a   b   c   d

6. What fractions are these arrows pointing to :-

   a 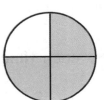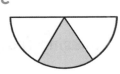   b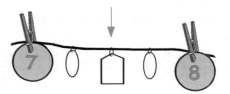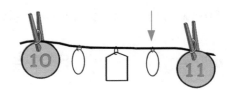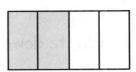

Tenths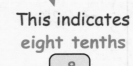

The washing line below has been split equally into 10 "bits".

Each "bit" is called one tenth.

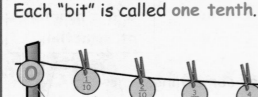

Can you see that
each bit
is one tenth ?

$\frac{1}{10}$

This indicates
eight tenths

$\frac{8}{10}$

Exercise 2

1. What fraction does each arrow point to here ?

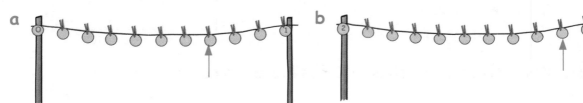

a   b

2. Write down the 3 missing fractions each time here :-

   a $\frac{3}{10}$, $\frac{4}{10}$, ..., ..., $\frac{7}{10}$, ...

   b $\frac{9}{10}$, ..., $\frac{7}{10}$, ..., ..., $\frac{4}{10}$.

3. Draw washing lines and show where each fraction would lie :-

   a $\frac{6}{10}$ b $2\frac{1}{10}$ c $7\frac{9}{10}$ d $3\frac{5}{10}$.

This number line has been split equally into 10 bits.

Each bit would be $\frac{1}{10}$.

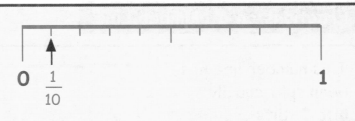

4. What fraction is indicated on this number line by each of the letters a, b, c and d ?

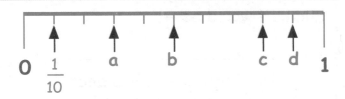

5. Look at this number line.

    e shows the fraction $5\frac{2}{10}$.

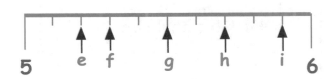

Write down what fraction is shown by f, g, h and i.

6. What fraction does each letter in these two diagrams stand for ?

7. Draw your own number line from 3 to 4, and split it into tenths.

    Indicate each of the following on your number line :-

    a $3\frac{1}{10}$ b $3\frac{5}{10}$ c $3\frac{7}{10}$ d $3\frac{9}{10}$.

    Worksheet 16·1

8. Draw number lines to show each of the following :-

    a $4\frac{2}{10}$ b $2\frac{5}{10}$ c $5\frac{1}{10}$ d $10\frac{8}{10}$.

9. The arrow in this diagram shows $\frac{4}{10}$.

    What is the fraction **three tenths** up from this ?

Identify where a basic fraction would be on a number line.

This number line has been split equally into **2** "bits".

0          $\frac{1}{2}$ 1

Each bit would be $\frac{1}{2}$.

This number line has been split equally into **4** bits.

Each bit would be $\frac{1}{4}$.

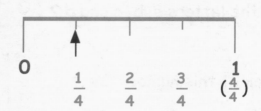

0          $\frac{1}{4}$ $\frac{2}{4}$ $\frac{3}{4}$ 1 $(\frac{4}{4})$

Each number line below has been split into equal bits.

3 equal bits

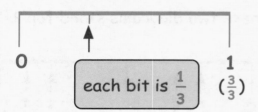

0   1

each bit is $\frac{1}{3}$ $(\frac{3}{3})$

5 equal bits

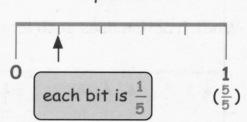

0   1

each bit is $\frac{1}{5}$ $(\frac{5}{5})$

6 equal bits

0   1

each bit is $\frac{1}{6}$ $\frac{5}{6}$

7 equal bits

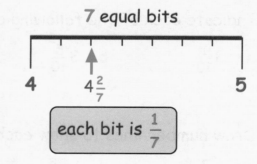

4          $4\frac{2}{7}$ 5

each bit is $\frac{1}{7}$

Can you see a pattern ?

8 equal bits .... each bit is $\frac{1}{8}$

9 equal bits .... each bit is $\frac{1}{9}$ ..... and so on ...

1. What **fraction** does each arrow point to on each of
    these number lines :–

    a

    0   1

    b

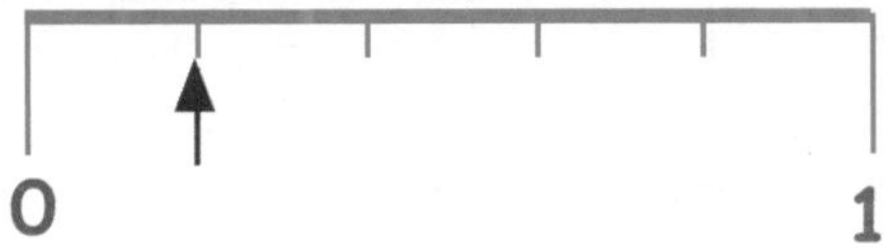

    0   1

    c

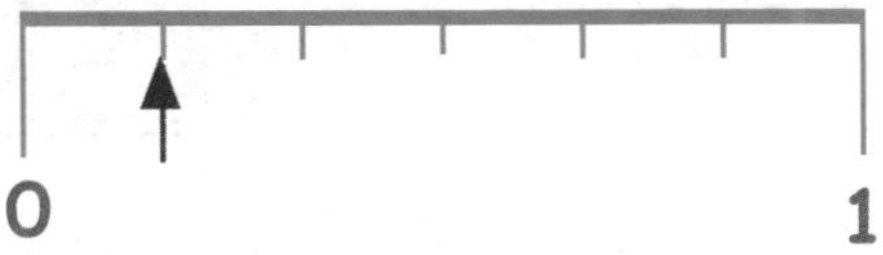

    0   1

    d

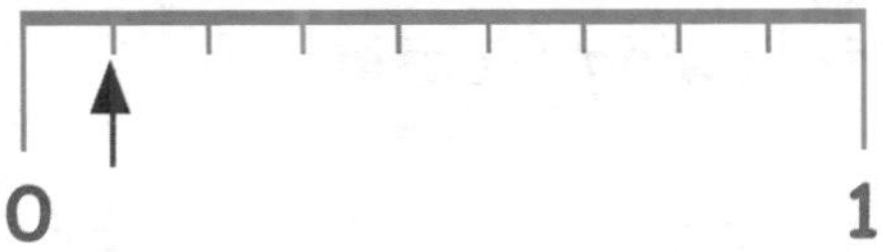

    0   1

    e

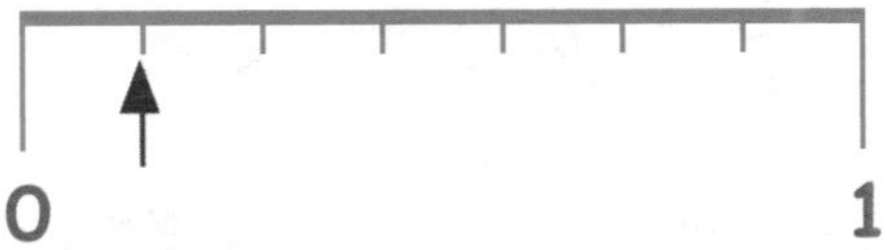

    0   1

    f

    0   1

This number line is
split into quarters.

The **arrow** is pointing to
3 and a three quarters. ($3\frac{3}{4}$).

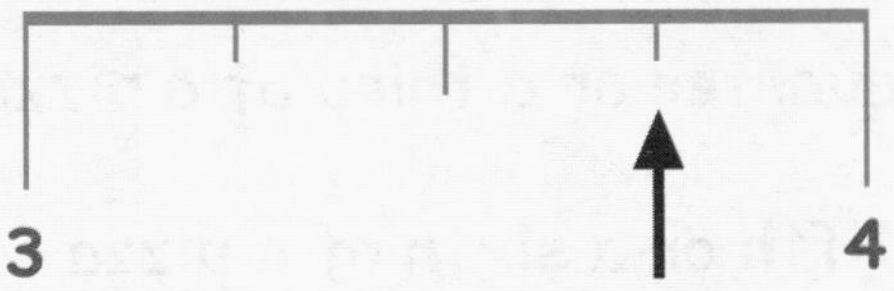

3   4

---

2. What **fraction** does each arrow represent :–

    a

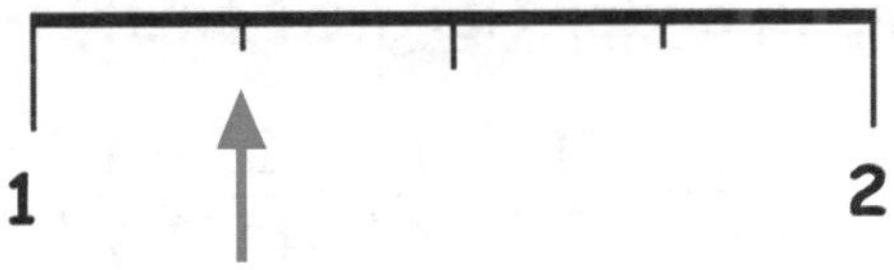

    1   2

    b

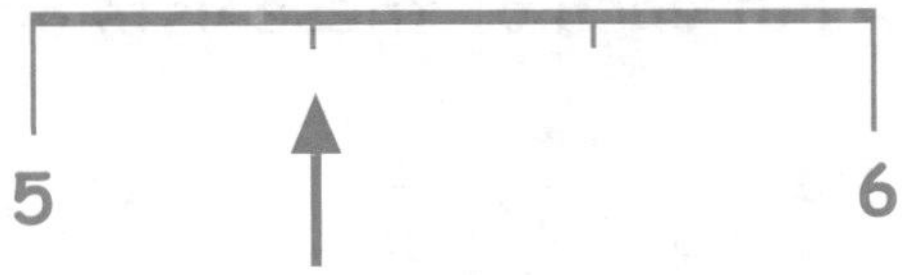

    5   6

    c

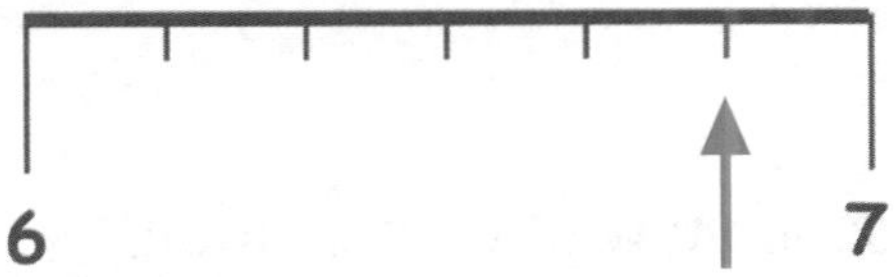

    6   7

    d

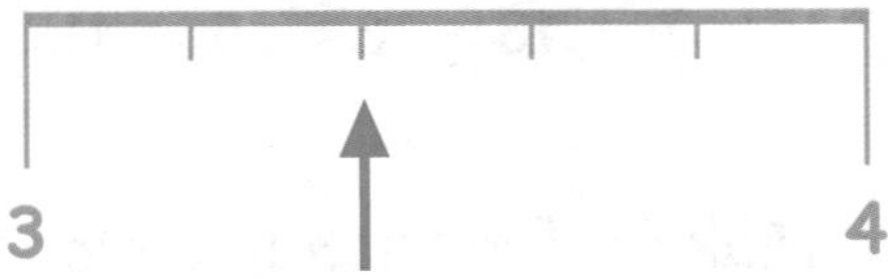

    3   4

    e

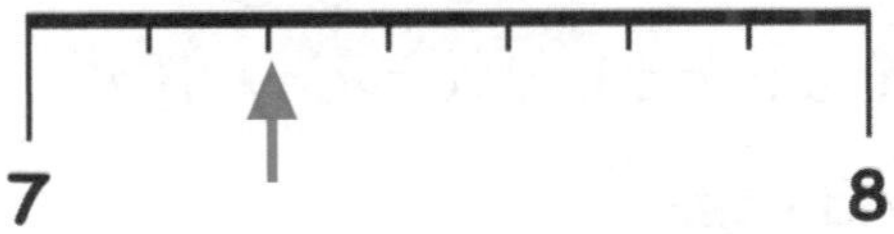

    7   8

    f

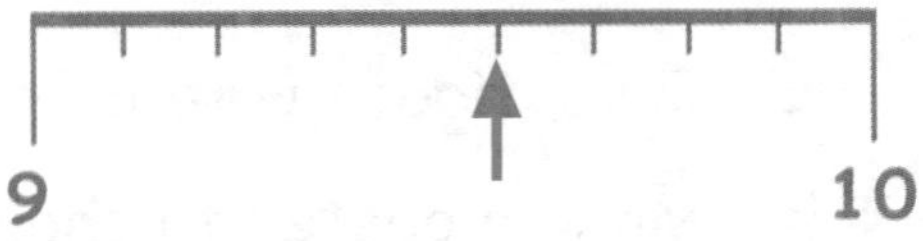

    9   10

2. g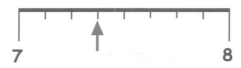

h

i

j

3. Draw number line diagrams to show each of the following fractions :-

a $6\frac{1}{2}$

b $2\frac{2}{3}$

c $2\frac{1}{5}$

d $3\frac{1}{6}$

e $5\frac{3}{4}$

f $1\frac{3}{5}$

g $3\frac{5}{6}$

h $4\frac{2}{5}$.

4. If you were *very* hungry, would you prefer :-

a   a half or a third of a pizza

b   a quarter or a third of a pizza

c   a fifth or a sixth of a pizza

d   an eighth or a ninth of a pizza ?

5. Put each of these lists of fractions in order (*largest* first) :-

a $\frac{1}{5}$, $\frac{1}{2}$, $\frac{1}{9}$

b $\frac{1}{5}$, $\frac{1}{4}$, $\frac{1}{10}$, $\frac{1}{7}$, $\frac{1}{100}$

c $\frac{1}{3}$, $\frac{1}{13}$, $\frac{1}{6}$, $\frac{1}{5}$, $\frac{1}{11}$

d   a tenth, $\frac{1}{3}$, an eighth, $\frac{1}{5}$.

6. Make a fraction line along the classroom wall or corridor.
   (*You could make a very big fraction line in the playground with chalk.*)

7. a   **Investigate** where fractions are used in everyday life.

   b   Make a poster to show your findings.

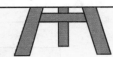

Be able to recognise what basic fraction of a shape is shaded.

Earlier we used :-

$\frac{1}{2}$ one part out of 2 parts.

$\frac{1}{3}$ one part out of 3 parts.

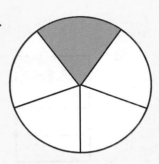

$\frac{1}{4}$ one part out of 4 parts.

This circle has split into 5 equal parts.

The red bit is "*one part out of 5*" parts.

This could be written as $\frac{1}{5}$.

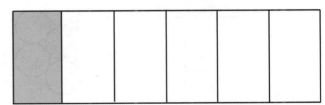

Exercise 4

1. This shape has 6 equal parts.
    What fraction is in pink.
    $\dfrac{1}{.....}$

2. Each circle below is split into equal parts.
    What fraction of each circle is coloured ?

a 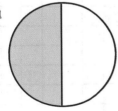   b 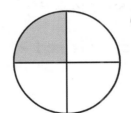   c 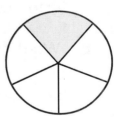   d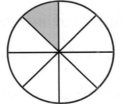

e    f 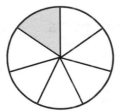   g 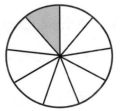   h

3. Each shape below is split into **equal** parts.

What **fraction** of each shape is **red**.

a
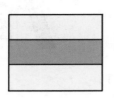

b
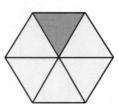

c
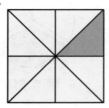

d
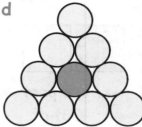

e
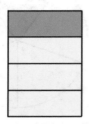

f
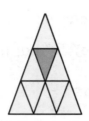

g
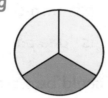

h
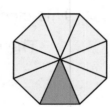

i
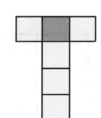

j
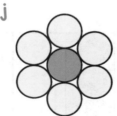

k
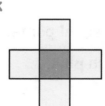

l
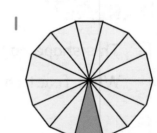

4. a   How many **squares** has this grid been split into ?

b   What fraction is **red** ?

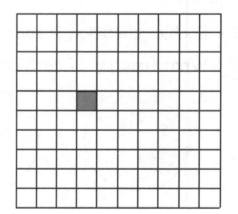

5. A **hexagon** is to be cut into 6 **equal** parts.

One part of the hexagon is to be **red**.

What **fraction** of the hexagon will be **red** ?

Identifying Fractions

Be able to identify a fraction of a shape.

A fraction consists of **2 parts** :-

$$\frac{2}{3}$$

the **DENOMINATOR** tells you the type of fraction you are dealing with (**thirds** here).

the **NUMERATOR** tells you the number or "how many" of the thirds (in this case **two**).

Example 1 :-

This shape shows **3** out of **4** equal parts are **green**.

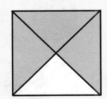

$\frac{3}{4}$ of this shape is **green**.

$\frac{1}{4}$ of this shape is **not green**.

Example 2 :-

This shape shows **3** out of **5** equal parts are **purple**.

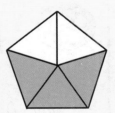

$\frac{3}{5}$ of this shape is **purple**.

$\frac{2}{5}$ of this shape is **not purple**.

Exercise 5

1. For each of the following, write the fraction that is coloured :-

a

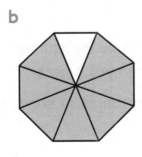

b

c

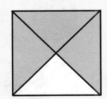

d

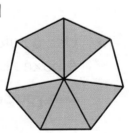

e

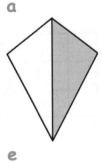

f

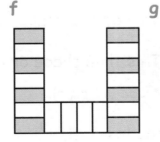

g

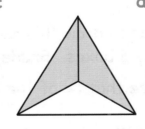

h

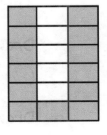

1. i   j   k   l

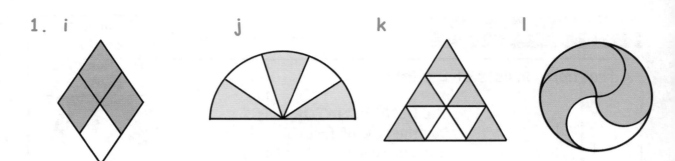

2. For each shape in Question 1, write what fraction is not coloured.

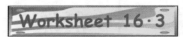

The picture shows 15 pieces of fruit.

(Can you see that 2 out of the 15 fruits are oranges, so $\frac{2}{15}$ are oranges ?)

3. Write down what fraction of the fruits are :-

a   bananas ($\frac{...}{15}$)   b   apples   c   plums   d   pears.

4. a   Use a ruler to draw this rectangle measuring
4 boxes by 3 boxes. Shade in any 5 boxes.
Can you see that $\frac{5}{12}$ of the rectangle is shaded ?

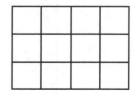

b   Draw the same box again.
This time shade or colour in $\frac{7}{12}$ of the shape.

c   Draw the same box again. This time shade or colour in $\frac{1}{6}$.
(*Hint : for every 6 equal parts shade in 1 part*).

d   Draw the box 3 times and shade :-   (i) $\frac{1}{3}$ (ii) $\frac{1}{4}$ (iii) $\frac{2}{3}$.

Revisit - Review - Revise

1. Find half of :-   a   12   b   36   c   120.

2. a   Trace or draw this rectangle.

   b   Colour in half of it **green**.

   c   Colour in a quarter of it blue.

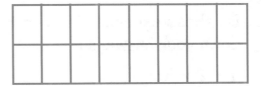

3. Write down the 3 missing fractions :- $\frac{2}{10}$, $\frac{3}{10}$,   ... ,   ... , $\frac{6}{10}$,   ...

4. What fraction does each arrow point to on these number lines ?

   a    b

   c    d

5. Draw number lines similar to those shown in Question 4 to show :-

   a $4\frac{1}{2}$ b $1\frac{3}{4}$ c $10\frac{4}{5}$.

6. What fraction of each shape is coloured ?

   a   b   c   d

   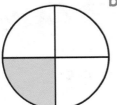      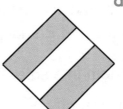

Chapter 17

Add, Subtract, Multiply and Divide Revision

Exercise 1

Be able to add and subtract up to 100 and to multiply and divide by 2, 5 and 10.

1. Do these examples in your head and write down your answers :-

a   2 x 10 = ...

b   35 ÷ 5 = ...

c   53 + 26 = ...

d   87 – 43 = ...

e   32 x 2 = ...

f   9 x 10 = ...

g   38 + 9 = ...

h   44 – 7 = ...

i   12 x 5 = ...

2. Copy and complete :-

a   46
   + 27
   ———

b   73
   – 26
   ———

c   19
   x 2
   ———

d   5)70

e   17
   x 5
   ———

f   2)57 .

3. Jill bought 2 bags of sweets. Each bag had 38 sweets.

   Roger bought 5 packets of sweets. Each packet had 13 sweets.

   a   How many sweets did Jill have in total ?

   b   How many sweets did Roger have in total ?

   c   (i)   Who had more sweets ?   (ii)   How many more ?

4. An eraser costs 19 pence. A sharpener costs 27 pence.

   a   What will it cost me altogether for 5 erasers and 2 sharpeners ?

   b   I bought them in a sale. I saved myself forty pence.

        What did I actually pay ?

   c   What would I pay for three erasers and a sharpener ?

This chapter gives you the chance to revise the 4 operations of mathematics which you have been introduced to - (+, ×, −, ÷).

You will have to recall how to add and subtract up to 1000 and how to multiply and divide by the numbers 2, 3, 4, 5, 8 and 10.

The early examples are set out, giving you clear instructions as to which operation you have to use.

Then you will meet problem type questions, when it will be up to you to decide which to use.

Be able to add and subtract up to 1000 and to multiply and divide by 2, 3, 4, 5, 8 and 10.

add ?
multiply ?
subtract ?
divide ?

Exercise 2

1. Do each of these examples in your head, then write down your answer.

   a $7 \times 3 = $ .....

   b $24 \div 2 = $ .....

   c $221 + 214 = $ ....

   d $32 - 16 = $ .....

   e $5 \times 8 = $ .....

   f $320 - 213 = $ ....

   g $314 + 118 = $ .....

   h $220 \div 5 = $ .....

   i $648 - 425 = $ ....

   j $475 + 436 = $ .....

   k $8 \times 12 = $ .....

   l $90 \div 10 = $ .....

   m $43 \times 5 = $ .....

   n $108 \div 4 = $ .....

   o $872 + 118 = $ .....

   p $690 - 287 = $ .....

   q $255 \div 5 = $ .....

   r $92 \times 3 = $ .....

   s $900 - 799 = $ .....

   t $886 - 775 = $ .....

   u $91 \times 8 = $ .....

   v $163 \div 8 = $ .....

   w $402 \div 5 = $ .....

   x $260 \div 10 = $ .....

2. Copy and complete :–

a
```
   817
 + 128
```

b
```
   914
 - 311
```

c
```
    47
  × 2
```

d 2 ⟌ 184

e
```
   609
 + 372
```

f
```
   425
 - 219
```

g
```
    34
   × 3
```

h 2 ⟌ 87

i
```
    66
   × 5
```

j
```
   951
 - 514
```

k
```
   378
 + 262
```

l 5 ⟌ 288

m
```
   436
 + 347
```

n 8 ⟌ 193

o
```
    27
   × 8
```

p
```
   768
 - 549
```

q
```
    37
   × 5
```

r
```
   573
 + 417
```

s 5 ⟌ 297

t
```
    77
   × 4
```

u 10 ⟌ 175

v
```
   629
 + 349
```

w
```
   891
 - 799
```

x 3 ⟌ 282

y
```
   683
 - 426
```

z
```
   448
 + 452
```

Be able to add or
subtract and multiply
or divide by 2, 3,
4, 5, 8 and 10.

In the following exercise, you have to
decide whether the problem involves
adding, subtracting, multiplying or dividing.

When you have decided, carry on and
solve the problem.

*Show all of
your working.*

Exercise 3

1. A school has 158 pupils in Year 1 and 135 pupils in Year 2.

    What is the total number of Year 1 and 2 pupils in the school ?

2.    There are 491 pupils in a school.

    272 of them are girls.

    How many boys are in the school ?

3. Tony sneezes 8 times a day.

    How many times did he sneeze in January ?

4. A multi-storey car park has 5 levels,
    each taking the same number of cars.

    When full, it holds 265 cars.

    How many cars can park on each level ?

5. The £288 raised at an event was split equally among 8 charities.

    How much did each charity get ?

6. Davie bought 150 chews. He ate 88 and gave 20 away.

    How many chews did he have left ?

7. There are 8 roller coasters at Pleasureland Park.

   Children from Stapleton Primary had spread themselves in groups of 18 to each ride.

   How many children from Stapleton Primary were there ?

8.  At a cricket match, there were 329 spectators in the North Stand and 487 in the South Stand.

   How many people in total were watching from the stands ?

9. One hundred and sixty four cyclists are registered in a race.

   45 of them withdraw before the start and 28 of them crashed.

   How many cyclists finished the race ?

10. Karen spent 4 days of her holidays stuck at home because of rain.

   She spent her time watching cars pass by.

   She counted 292 cars in 4 days. (Same number each day).

   How many cars passed each day ?

11. A city has 8 hotels. In each hotel there are 87 workers.

    How many hotel workers are there in that city ?

12. Jo has 2 books of 100 stickers, 3 books of 10 stickers and 4 single stickers.

    How many stickers does she have altogether ?

13.  3 apes ate 32 bananas each day for 4 days.

    How many bananas were eaten altogether ?

14.

A farmer had 150 mother pigs.

In summer 90 of them had 6 piglets each, while the rest each had 5 piglets.

How many piglets were born that summer ?

15. Three trains left London just after 10 am.

The Southampton train left with 158 passengers on board.

The Leeds train had 173 and the train to Carlisle carried 97.

a   How many passengers altogether were on these three trains ?

The 10.30 am train to Birmingham had one quarter of the total of the above three trains.

b   How many passengers were on the Birmingham train ?

16. A flock of eight swallows flew 78 miles south to escape the cold.

After resting, they flew another 20 miles towards the coast.

a   How many miles did each swallow fly ?

b   How many miles did the eight of them fly altogether ?

17. Three hotels are busy with bookings for Christmas dinner.

- · Holton's have taken bookings for 152 people.
- · Latella's have 126 booked.
- · Spice Rack expect 64 people.

a   What is the total number of people booked at these hotels ?

b   Last year, each hotel had only a half of this year's bookings.

What was the difference in the total number of bookings between this year and last year at this time ?

1. Find :-

   a $5 \times 2 = \ldots$

   b $246 \div 3 = \ldots$

   c $224 + 116 = \ldots$

   d $376 - 145 = \ldots$

   e $8 \times 47 = \ldots$

   f $541 - 222 = \ldots$

   g $235 \div 5 = \ldots$

   h $120 \div 8 = \ldots$

   i $707 - 558 = \ldots$

   j $172 \div 4 = \ldots$

   k $67 \times 4 = \ldots$

   l $170 \div 10 = \ldots$

2. Copy and complete :-

   a $\begin{array}{r} 724 \\ + 128 \\ \hline \end{array}$

   b $\begin{array}{r} 872 \\ - 587 \\ \hline \end{array}$

   c $\begin{array}{r} 85 \\ \times 4 \\ \hline \end{array}$

   d $8\overline{)128}$

   e $\begin{array}{r} 76 \\ \times 3 \\ \hline \end{array}$

   f $5\overline{)265}$

   g $\begin{array}{r} 650 \\ - 467 \\ \hline \end{array}$

   h $2\overline{)157}$

   i $\begin{array}{r} 39 \\ \times 8 \\ \hline \end{array}$

3. a   There are 272 paintings in a gallery.

   Forty three are landscape,

   76 are portraits, the rest are modern art.

   How many modern art paintings are there ?

   b   Davie has 32 marbles.

   Jack has eight times as many as Davie.

   Tony has half as many as Jack.

   How many marbles does Tony have ?

Representing Fractions Revision

Represent fractions on a number line.

Exercise 1

1. What fraction does each arrow point to ?

2. What fraction is represented by each arrow ?

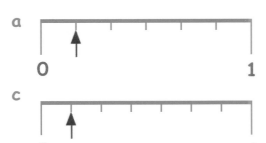

3. What fraction of each shape is coloured blue ?

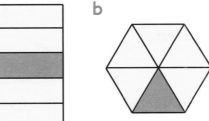

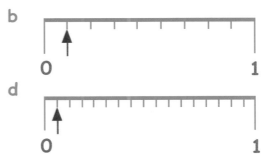

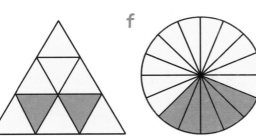

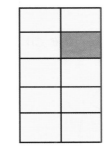

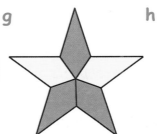

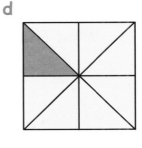

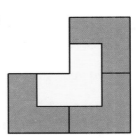

4. What fraction of each shape in Question 3 is not coloured blue ?

Be able to find an equivalent fraction.

This rectangle has been divided up in TWO different ways.

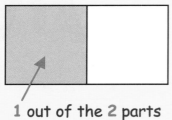

1 out of the 2 parts is shaded pink $= \dfrac{1}{2}$

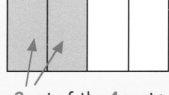

2 out of the 4 parts are shaded pink $= \dfrac{2}{4}$

Can you see from the diagrams that the two fractions $\dfrac{1}{2}$ and $\dfrac{2}{4}$ are the SAME ?

These are called **equivalent** fractions.

$$\dfrac{2}{4} = \dfrac{1}{2}$$

Exercise 2

1. This circle has been divided into **3** equal parts.

   a   What fraction of the circle is coloured **blue** ?

   b 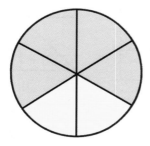   The same circle has been divided into **6** parts this time.

   What fraction this time is coloured **blue** ?

   *Can you see that identical parts of the circle have been coloured **blue** both times ?*

   c   **Copy** this sentence and finish it :-

   "The 2 diagrams show the fractions $\dfrac{2}{3} = \dfrac{\dots}{6}$ are **equivalent**".

2. Use the two drawings opposite to write down the 2 fractions that are shown to be **equivalent** to each other.

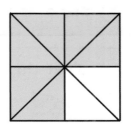
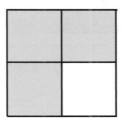

i.e. $\dfrac{3}{4}$ = ...

3. Use each pair of drawings below to write down the 2 fractions that are shown to be **equivalent** to each other.

a

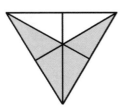

b

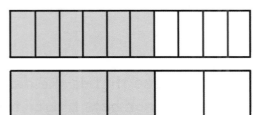

c

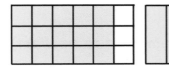

d

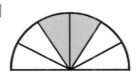

e

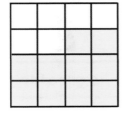

f

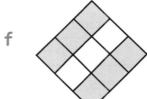
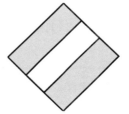

4. Draw or trace both of these squares.

a   In the first one, colour in **2** boxes.

b   What **fraction** have you shaded ?

c   Colour in the correct number of boxes in your 2nd square so that both shapes look the same.

d   Use your drawings to **complete** :- $\dfrac{...}{3}$ = $\dfrac{?}{6}$.

Worksheet 18·1

Comparing and Ordering Fractions

Be able to compare and order basic fractions.

Look at the fractions of pizza below.

$\dfrac{1}{2}$ $\dfrac{1}{3}$ $\dfrac{1}{4}$ $\dfrac{1}{5}$

Can you see that as the denominator (*number on the bottom*) of the fraction gets bigger the fraction itself gets smaller ?

Exercise 3

1. a   List these fractions in order of size (*from largest to smallest*) :-

$$\frac{1}{4}\,,\quad \frac{1}{2}\,,\quad \frac{1}{5}\,,\quad \frac{1}{3}$$

   b   This time, list them from smallest to largest.

Remember :- < means "is smaller than" and > means "is greater than".

---

2. Copy each pair of fractions below and insert "<", ">" or "=" :-

   a $\dfrac{1}{4}$ ..... $\dfrac{1}{2}$ b $\dfrac{1}{5}$ ..... $\dfrac{1}{3}$ c $\dfrac{1}{2}$ ..... $\dfrac{1}{5}$ d $\dfrac{1}{2}$ ..... $\dfrac{2}{4}$

   e $\dfrac{1}{5}$ ..... $\dfrac{1}{6}$ f $\dfrac{1}{3}$ ..... $\dfrac{2}{3}$ g $\dfrac{3}{4}$ ..... $\dfrac{1}{4}$ h $\dfrac{1}{18}$ ..... $\dfrac{1}{17}$.

3. Write each set of fractions below in order (*largest to smallest*) :-

   a $\dfrac{1}{5},\ \dfrac{1}{2},\ \dfrac{1}{8},\ \dfrac{1}{4},$ b $\dfrac{1}{4},\ \dfrac{1}{5},\ \dfrac{2}{4},\ \dfrac{1}{6},\ \dfrac{1}{10},\ \dfrac{1}{3}$

   c   a half, a quarter, a ninth, a third, a sixth, a fifth, a fifteenth.

Adding and Subtracting (basic) Fractions

Be able to add or subtract basic fractions.

If you had **1** quarter piece of pizza and someone gave you another **2** quarters of pizza you would have **3** quarter pieces of pizza.

This sum can be written as :-

$$\frac{1}{4} + \frac{2}{4} = \frac{3}{4}.$$

Example 1 :-

$$\frac{2}{5} + \frac{1}{5} = \frac{3}{5}$$

Example 2 :-

$$\frac{4}{7} - \frac{1}{7} = \frac{3}{7}$$

Example 3 :-

$$\frac{7}{10} - \frac{6}{10} = \frac{1}{10}$$

Exercise 4

1. Find :-

   a $\frac{1}{4} + \frac{1}{4}$ b $\frac{2}{5} + \frac{2}{5}$ c $\frac{3}{5} + \frac{1}{5}$ d $\frac{5}{8} + \frac{1}{8}$

   e $\frac{3}{4} - \frac{1}{4}$ f $\frac{3}{10} - \frac{1}{10}$ g $\frac{15}{16} - \frac{7}{16}$ h $\frac{11}{75} - \frac{10}{75}.$

2. Find :-   a $\frac{3}{4} + \frac{1}{4}$ b $\frac{3}{5} + \frac{2}{5}$ c $\frac{3}{10} + \frac{7}{10}.$

3. Can you see that the answers to all Question **2** is always **1** ?

4. I have 4 whole pizzas and a third of a pizza.
   Paul gave me another third of a pizza.
   How much pizza do I have now ?

   $$4\frac{1}{3} + \frac{1}{3} = 4\frac{...}{3}$$

5. Find :- a $5\frac{1}{3} + \frac{1}{3}$ b $8\frac{1}{4} + \frac{1}{4}$ c $6\frac{3}{5} - \frac{1}{5}$

   d $2\frac{1}{2} - 1\frac{1}{2}$ e $3\frac{3}{7} + 2\frac{1}{7}$ f $5\frac{3}{4} - 2\frac{1}{4}.$

1. What fraction is indicated by each arrow ?

    a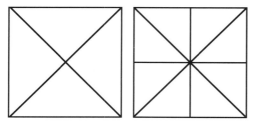

    b

2. Draw or trace both circles.

    a Colour or shade both circles to show that a half equals two quarters.

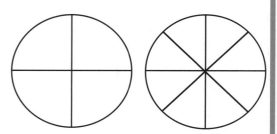

    b

    Draw or trace both squares.

    Colour or shade the 2 squares to show that $\frac{3}{4} = \frac{6}{8}$.

3. Copy and complete these equivalent fractions :-

    a $\frac{1}{2} = \frac{...}{4}$

    b $\frac{2}{3} = \frac{...}{6}$

    c $\frac{4}{5} = \frac{...}{10}$

4. Put each group of fractions in order, largest first :-

    a $\frac{1}{2}$, $\frac{1}{10}$, $\frac{1}{4}$, $\frac{1}{11}$

    b $\frac{1}{5}$, sixth, $\frac{2}{4}$, ninth, $\frac{1}{12}$.

5. Copy each pair of fractions below and insert "<", ">" or "=" :-

    a $\frac{1}{3}$ ..... $\frac{1}{2}$

    b $\frac{1}{3}$ ..... $\frac{1}{5}$

    c $\frac{1}{10}$ ..... $\frac{1}{3}$

    d $\frac{2}{4}$ ..... $\frac{1}{2}$.

6. Find :-

    a $\frac{1}{3} + \frac{1}{3}$

    b $\frac{2}{5} + \frac{1}{5}$

    c $\frac{3}{8} - \frac{1}{8}$

    d $3\frac{3}{4} - 1\frac{1}{4}$.

1. Write these numbers using **digits** :-

    a   two hundred and thirty   b   six hundred and eighty five.

2. Write these numbers **in words** :-

    a   78   b   409   c   753   d   999.

3. Write the number that comes :-

    a   just **after** 149   b   100 **before** 730   c   ten **after** 360.

4. In the number **387**, what does the digit :-

    a   **7** stand for   b   **8** stand for   c   **3** stand for ?

5. State whether A, B and C are **right**, **acute** or **obtuse** angles :-

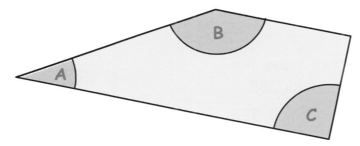

6. How many **right angles** are there in :-

    a   a half turn   b   a quarter turn   c   a complete turn ?

7. a   What colour of line is **parallel** to the blue line ?

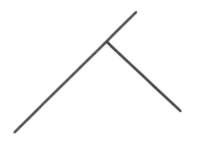

    b   What colour of line is **perpendicular** to the blue line ?

8. Tommy is looking up at the flagpole.

    In real life, is a flagpole sitting in a **vertical** or **horizontal** position ?

9. Imagine a clock is to show a time of **9:20**.

    What **type** of angle will there be between the two hands on the clock ?

    (*right, acute* or *obtuse*)

10. **Copy** and **work out** :-

    a   35
         + 9

    b   7
         + 58

    c   74
         + 27

    d   67
         + 43

    e   254
         + 589

    f   64
         + 728

    g   594
         + 267

    h   387
         + 526

11. I walked **229** metres along one edge of a triangular field, **85** metres along the second edge, then **168** metres along the 3rd edge, back to my starting point.

    How far did I walk in **total** ?

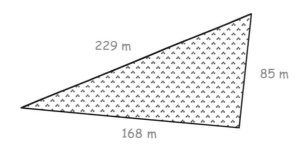

229 m   85 m   168 m

12. Write down the months of the year in **reverse** order.

    Start with December, Nov......, ..., ...

13. Copy these **Roman** numerals and fill in the missing numbers :-

III,	IV,	......,	VI,	......,	VIII,	......,	X,	......,	XII.

14. Write each of these times in 2 ways. (e.g. 7:35 or twenty five to eight)

a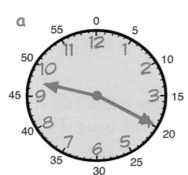

b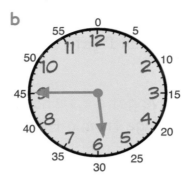

c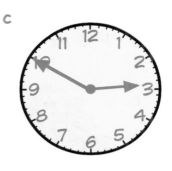

15. Write each time below in 12 hour form using am or pm :-

   a   half past 6 in the morning   b   quarter to ten at night.

16. Work out :-

   a   57   b   347   c   569   d   908
       - 34   -   35   - 247   - 405

   e   53   f   526   g   758   h   802
       -   9   -   68   - 479   - 507

17. Find :-

   a   79 – 26   b   504 – 85   c   428 – 259   d   737 – 588.

18. Three boys were comparing their stamp collections.

   Terry had 362 stamps.
   James had 184 stamps.
   Nick had 197 stamps.

   a   How many stamps altogether ?

   b   How many more stamps had Terry than Nick ?

19. a How many **20p** coins can I get for a **£5** note ?

    b How many **50p** coins can I get for a **£50** note ?

20. a  Dave got a **£10** note, a **£5** note and a **20p** coin as change from a **£20** note, when he bought a comic.

    How much must the comic have cost ?

    b What notes and coins might Jill have used to pay for her new jacket **exactly**, which cost **£37** and **75p** ?

    c Billy handed over a **£20** note and received **£3** and **55p** for his petrol which cost **£15** and **45p**.

    Had Billy been given the correct change ? (*Explain*).

21. a Measure both the **length** and the **width** of this rectangle in **millimetres**.

length

breadth

    b Calculate the **perimeter** of the rectangle.

22. a Shown is a sketch of a right angled triangle.
       Make an accurate drawing of the triangle.

    b Measure the length of the 3rd side.

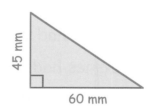

45 mm

60 mm

23.  If you were asked to measure the length of a **real** umbrella handle, would you measure it in **millimetres**, **centimetres** or **metres** ?

24. To make a model of this cuboid, you would need 6 pieces of card, all of them rectangles.

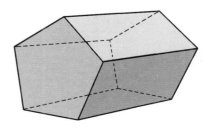

Say what 2-D shapes you would need to make each of these two shapes :-

a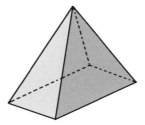

b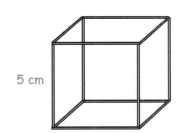

25. What total length of straws would you need to build this model of a cube ?

5 cm

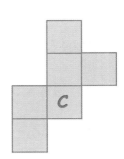

26. Which of these nets would make a cube ?

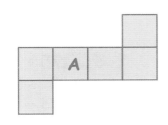   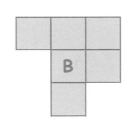

A   B   C

27. Copy and complete :-

a   37
    × 3

b   82
    × 2

c   66
    × 5

d   87
    × 4

e   36
    × 10

f   72
    × 8

g   69
    × 4

h   33
    × 8 .

28. What numbers are missing ?

a 4 × .... = 44   b .... × 5 = 45   c 8 × .... = 72   d ... × 10 = 310.

29. Copy and work out :-

     a   2)76   b   3)96   c   10)85   d   5)80

     e   4)136   f   5)215   g   8)280   h   3)258 .

30. Find :-

a	$39 \div 2$	b	$177 \div 3$	c	$248 \div 4$	d	$195 \div 5$
e	$128 \div 8$	f	$220 \div 10$	g	$256 \div 8$	h	$300 \div 4.$

31. TeeJay textbooks are packed into boxes.

Each box holds 8 books.

How many boxes are needed to hold
240 books ?

32. Find :-

a	$49 \div 5$	b	$277 \div 4$	c	$151 \div 3$	d	$175 \div 2$
e	$322 \div 4$	f	$210 \div 8$	g	$276 \div 10$	h	$123 \div 5.$

33. a   What is the day just after Sunday ?

     b   Which day comes 2 days before Saturday ?

     c   Which month comes 2 months after November ?

34. a   How many days are there in March ?

     b   How many days are there in a leap year ?

35. a   Write the date 03/08/14 out fully in words.

     b   Write the date June 15th 2016 in number form.

36. Use **tally marks** to show the numbers :- a 13   b 29.

37. A group was asked to name their favourite top-of-the-range car.

Rolls Royce	Jaguar	Porsche	Jaguar	Ferrari
Ferrari	Rolls Royce	Ferrari	Porsche	Maserati
Jaguar	Porsche	Rolls Royce	Lamborghini	Jaguar
Maserati	Ferrari	Ferrari	Maserati	Ferrari
Porsche	Maserati	Ferrari	Porsche	Lamborghini
Jaguar	Ferrari	Rolls Royce	Ferrari	Porsche

a **Copy** and **complete** the tally table.

b How many said Rolls Royce ?

c How many **more** chose Porsche than Lamborghini ?

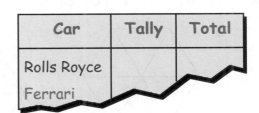

Car	Tally	Total
Rolls Royce		
Ferrari		

d Draw a neat labelled **bar chart** to show all this information.

38. People at the cinema were asked what drink they chose to take in.

The table lists their replies :-

cola	fanta	lemonade	water	coffee
water	cola	fanta	water	fanta
fanta	water	cola	lemonade	cola
cola	cola	water	cola	lemonade

a **Copy** and **complete** the tally table.

b How many chose **cola** ?

c Draw a **pictograph** to show the information.

Drink	Tally	Total
cola		
fanta		

Use [ ] to represent 2 drinks.

Remember to label your diagram.

39. Find **half** of :-   a   14   b   28   c   236.

40. Find a **quarter** of :- a   20   b   56   c   132.

41. What **fraction** does each arrow point to on these number lines ?

a
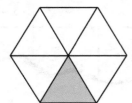

b

42. What **fraction** of each shape is coloured ?

a   b   c   d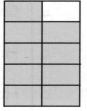

43. Copy and complete to show these **equivalent** fractions :-

a $\frac{1}{2} = \frac{...}{6}$ b $\frac{1}{4} = \frac{2}{...}$ c $\frac{2}{5} = \frac{...}{10}$.

44. Write these fractions in order, **smallest first** :- $\frac{1}{8}$, $\frac{1}{5}$, $\frac{1}{12}$, $\frac{1}{3}$.

45. Find :-

a $\frac{1}{5} + \frac{3}{5}$ b $\frac{5}{8} - \frac{3}{8}$ c $\frac{1}{4} + \frac{3}{4}$ d $2\frac{5}{6} - \frac{1}{6}$.

46. Find mentally :-

a 5×4 = ...   b $224 \div 4$ = ...   c $317 + 254$ = ...

d $587 - 243$ = ...   e 8×32 = ...   f $545 - 222$ = ...

g $225 \div 3$ = ...   h $120 \div 8$ = ...   i 10×85 = ...

j $245 \div 5$ = ...   k 53×4 = ...   l $900 \div 10$ = ...

47. For each question here, decide whether to add, subtract, multiply or divide, then set down the working neatly and find the answer :-

a   A truck tyre weighs **45** kilograms.

     What does a set of **4** tyres weigh ?

b    The distance by road from London to Manchester is **319** kilometres.

     From Manchester to Glasgow is a further **344** kilometres.

     What is the **total** driving distance from London to Glasgow via Manchester ?

c   A local cinema charges **£8** per ticket to see a film.

     Last night, the takings were **£288**.

     How many people watched last night's film ?

d    The sugar and the flour together in a cake mix weighed **750** grams.

     The flour itself weighed **480** grams.

     How much sugar was used ?

48. Copy and complete these additions and subtractions :-

a   420 grams
     + 260 grams
     ⎯⎯⎯⎯⎯⎯

b   830 ml
     – 690 ml
     ⎯⎯⎯⎯

c   3 kg   200 g
     + 4 kg   500 g
     ⎯⎯⎯⎯⎯⎯⎯⎯

49. When Mirin put her turkey into the oven, it had a mass of 3 kg 750 grams.

After it had been cooked, the turkey then had a mass of 2 kg 300 grams.

How much had it lost in mass during cooking ?

Ch 0 - Revision - Page 1

1. a 28, 30, 32, ... 36
   b 70, 65, 60, ..., 50
2. 79
3. 61
4. A = 29, B = 37
5. a 69   b 77   c 78   d 86
6. 58 (or 91)
7. a 29   b 97   c 87   d 99
8. 90
9. 5 or 7 if external angles included
10. a 51   b 42   c 56   d 38
11. 13
12. a 5   b 54   c 53   d 60
13. 73
14. chair, hut, tube train, house, cathedral
15. wine glass, teapot, sink, bath, pond, lake.
16. a no   b yes   c yes
    d no   e no   f yes
17. a rectangle   b triangle
    c square   d circle
18. square - 9   rectangle - 7
    circle - 5   triangle - 5
19. a 1   b 3   c 4   d 4
20. various
21. a 36   b 83   c 74   d 92
22. 97
23. a 25   b 82   c 95   d 82
24. 94
25. a 17   b 45   c 67   d 58
26. 47
27. a 18   b 15   c 35   d 89
28. 48
29. a 50p, 20p, 2p, 1p
    b £2, 20p, 10p, 5p, 2p
    c £10, £2, 50p, 20p
30. £6 and 10p
31. a £6   b £7 and 60p
32. a 10   b 16   c 8   d 12
    e 24   f 20   g 14   h 18
33. a 36   b 74   c 30   d 96
    e 78   f 54   g 92   h 50
34. 94p
35. a square
    b Rectangle, Rhombus
    c Parallelogram
    d kite   e square   f kite

36. a Sunday, Monday, Tuesday, Wednesday, Thursday, Friday, Saturday
    b Jan, Feb, Mar, Apr, May, Jun, Aul, Aug, Sep, Oct, Nov, Dec
37. a 10·20 or 20 past 10
    b 10·45 or quarter to 11
    c 12·40 or 20 to 1
38. a 35   b 30   c 40   d 70
    e 45   f 60   g 55   h 90
39. a 80   b 78   c 80   d 95
    e 70   f 96   g 54   h 120
40. 90
41. 35p + 24p + 20p = 79p
42. a cylinder   b squ pyramid
    c cube   d prism
43. a 6   b 12   c 6   d 8
44. a 23   b 17 r 1
    c 36 r 1   d 47 r 1
    e 14   f 35
    g 46 r 1   h 34 r 1
45. 8 each with 1 left over
46. a 7   b 8
    c 15   d 16 r 2
    e 7   f 12
    g 9 r 1   h 10 r 6
    i 9   j 13 r 2
    k 9   l 4 r 3
47. 19
48. a quarter   b half
    c third   d 3 quarters
49. any two bits coloured
50. 21 cows
51. forward 3, turn left
    forward 3, turn right
    forward 2, turn right
    forward 2, turn left
    forward 2
42. a rabbit   b duck
    c meerkat
53. a Dinner - 10   b 6   c 26
54. a £26   b £58
55. a 4   b 16   c 4   d 44
56. a 9 cm by 2 cm   b 7 cm
57. a m   b cm   c m   d m
58. a 8p   b 13 g   c £17
59. a 7$\frac{1}{2}$ b 10$\frac{3}{4}$
60. 4$\frac{1}{4}$, 4, 3$\frac{3}{4}$, 3$\frac{1}{2}$

61. a 14   b 9   c 79
    d 77   e 54   f 60
62. a 47   b 29   c 30
    d 17   e 90   f 37 r 1
63. a 68p   b 12p
64. a ⦀⦀ ⦀⦀⦀
    b ⦀⦀⦀ ⦀⦀⦀ ⦀⦀⦀ ⦀⦀⦀ ⦀⦀⦀ ⦀⦀
65.

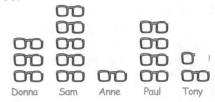

Donna   Sam   Anne   Paul   Tony

66. a

No.	Tally Marks	How Many
1	⦀⦀⦀ ⦀⦀⦀⦀	9
2	⦀⦀⦀ ⦀⦀⦀ ⦀	11
3	⦀⦀⦀ ⦀	6
4	⦀⦀⦀⦀	4

   b 9   c 30
   d graph

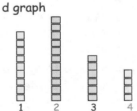

   1   2   3   4

67. a grams   b kg
68. a millilitres   b litres

Ch 1 - Whole Numbers - Page 13

Ch 1 - Exercise 1 - Page 13

1. 1 ten and 5 units
2. a 1 ten 4 units   b 2 and 6
   c 3 and 7   d 8 and 1
   e 6 and 3   f 9 and 0
   g 0 and 7   h 7 and 9
3. a 7   b 6
4. a 9   b 5
5. 2 hundreds, 3 tens and 7 units
6. a 4 hundreds, 1 ten and 8 units
   b 6 hundreds, 5 tens and 7 units
   c 9 hundreds, 0 tens and 2 units
   d 8 hundreds, 9 tens and 2 units
   e 7 hundreds, 6 tens and 0 units

7. a 3 hundreds, 0 tens and 0 units
   b 7 hundreds, 2 tens and 7 units
   c 6 hundreds, 0 tens and 2 units
   d 9 hundreds, 3 tens and 0 units
   e 2 hundreds, 7 tens and 5 units
   f 3 hundreds, 8 tens and 4 units
   g 7 hundreds, 1 ten and 7 units
   h 9 hundreds, 8 tens and 9 units
   i 1 hundred, 7 tens and 2 units
   j 6 hundreds, 5 tens and 8 units
   k 2 hundreds, 8 tens and 4 units
   l 5 hundreds, 4 tens and 7 units
8. a 3 and 4   b 6 and 3
   c 9 and 6   d 4 and 5
   e 8 and 8   f 5 and 7
   g 5 and 0   h 7 and 0
   i 10 and 0
9. a 174   b 248   c 620   d 582
   e 45   f 180   g 978
10. £4 and 39p
11. £6 and 75p

Ch 1 - Exercise 2 - *Page 16*

1. a 28   b 38   c 45
   d 71   e 67   f 50
   g 12   h 80   i 59
2. a 117   b 243   c 564   d 326
   e 855   f 714   g 970   h 667
   i 808   j 999
3. a sixty eight   b forty two
   c thirty six   d eighteen
   e seventy   f ninety five
   g one hundred and seventy eight
   h three hundred and nineteen
   i nine hundred and eleven
   j five hundred and four
   k eight hundred
   l a thousand
4. a 42   b 75   c 83   d 627
   e 950   f 639   g 789   h 799
5. a 35   b 89   c 50   d 110
   e 877   f 699   g 621   h 1000
6. a 60   b 120   c 195   d 215
   e 300   f 523   g 804   h 1001
7. a 80   b 130   c 185   d 300
   e 425   f 543   g 795   h 891
8. a 300   b 450   c 520   d 595
   e 601   f 856   g 990   h 1000
9. a 200   b 150   c 290   d 350
   e 520   f 595   g 710   h 900
10. position 429
11. a 511, 453, 388, 302, 297

b 452, 428, 301, 234, 175
c 857, 800, 703, 578, 519
d 625, 562, 526, 265, 256
12. a 16, 17, 23, 31
    b 72, 77, 81, 85, 90
    c 106, 114, 140, 165, 172
    d 259, 295, 499, 501, 581
    e 330, 357, 389, 403, 430
    f 567, 576, 657, 675, 756
13. a The poplar tree
    b The rowan tree
    c The willow tree
    d The beech tree
14. a 49   b 54   c 102   d 107
    e 181   f 189   g 629   h 642
    i 943   j 955   k 966
15. a 17   b 73   c 298
16. 726
17. six hundred and seven
18. a four hundred and twenty seven
      centimetres
    b forty six kilograms

Ch 2 - Angles - *Page 21*

Ch 2 - Exercise 1 - *Page 21*

1. a right b right   c smaller
   d bigger e right   f right
2. a 9   b 8
3. smaller - a, b, e, i, j,
   bigger - c, d, f, g, h, k
   right - l, m
4. a 3, 6, 7   b 2, 4   c 1, 5

Ch 2 - Exercise 3 - *Page 23*

1. a right b acute c obtuse
   d obtuse e right f acute
2. a right b obtuse c acute
   d acute e right f acute
3. a blue is obtuse
     yellow is obtuse
     purple is acute
     red is acute
     green is acute
   b an acute angle
4. right - 3, 6, 7
   acute - 1, 5
   obtuse - 2, 4
5. a right b obtuse c acute
   d acute e acute   f obtuse
6. various
7. reflex

Ch 2 - Exercise 3 - *Page 25*

1. a 1   b 2   c 4
2. a 1   b 2   c 1
   d 2   e 3   f 4
3. a 1   b 2   c 1
   d 3   e 1   f 4
4. a 1   b 2   c 3
   d 1   e 3   f 1
5. a quarter turn clockwise or a
     3 quarter turn anticlockwise.
   b half turn clockwise or a
     half turn anticlockwise.
   c full turn clockwise or a
     full turn anticlockwise.
   d 3 quarter turn clockwise or a
     quarter turn anticlockwise.
   e 3 quarter turn clockwise or a
     quarter turn anticlockwise.
   f quarter turn clockwise or a
     3 quarter turn anticlockwise.

Ch 2 - Exercise 4 - *Page 27*

1. a A   b E
   c C and F
   d A and E
2. a yes   b yes   c yes
3. yes
4. square, rhombus, parallelogram
5. a various   b various
6. two sets, blue and green
7. a cube has 3 sets
   b prism has 4 sets
   c pyramid has 2 sets
8 Investigation

Ch 3 - Addition - *Page 30*

Ch 3 - Exercise 1 - *Page 30*

1. a 23   b 57   c 39   d 89
   e 96   f 97   g 79   h 88
   i 99   j 59   k 69   l 95
2. a 48   b 77   c 58   d 88
   e 99   f 33   g 69   h 67
3. 65 m
4. 79
5. 57
6. 88
7. 89
8. 97

Ch 3 - Exercise 2 - *Page 32*

1. a 71   b 74   c 72   d 85
   e 90   f 90   g 95   h 91
   i 60   j 93   k 94   l 100
2. a 93   b 84   c 50   d 87
   e 92   f 82   g 95   h 100
   i 99   j 61   k 84   l 70
3. 43 fish
4. 92 pennies
5. 64 cards
6. 46 questions
7. a 82   b 98
8. a 72p   b 91p

Ch 3 - Exercise 3 - *Page 34*

1. a 107   b 489   c 349   d 598
   e 897   f 797   g 749   h 898
   i 978   j 979   k 987   l 889
2. a 587   b 679   c 498   d 689
   e 500   f 779   g 793   h 699
   i 688   j 887   k 948   l 987
   m 886   n 998   o 901   p 1000

Ch 3 - Exercise 4 - *Page 35*

1. a 243   b 566   c 790   d 885
   e 921   f 615   g 911   h 876
   i 910   j 810   k 986   l 1000
2. a 580   b 564   c 795   d 568
   e 600   f 810   g 665   h 545
   i 976   j 277   k 930   l 910
3. £950
4. 410
5. £944
6. 951 trees
7. a chair b £517 c £616
8. Yasmin - 361, Trevor - 369,
   Micky - 483 - Micky won
9. £515
10. 431 workers
11. 921 pages
12. 691 birds
13. a 265p   b 456p   c 721p
14. 622 pencils
15. 700 fish
16. 621 bees
17. 600 g
18. 565 km
19. 605 bricks
20. 433 beans

Ch 3 - Exercise 5 - *Page 39*

1. a 29   b 45   c 97   d 130
   e 227   f 771   g 482   h 845
2. a 146   b 498   c 910   d 980
3. 316 runs
4. 119 bits
5. 28 choices
6. a 167   b 287   c 520
   d 584   e 526   f 437

Ch 4 - Time 1 - *Page 41*

Ch 4 - Exercise 1 - *Page 41*

1. a Monday, Tuesday, Wednesday,
   Thursday, Friday, Saturday
   Sunday
   b January, February, March,
   April, May, June
   July, August, September
   October, November, December
2. a Monday   b Saturday
3. a 5 o'clock   b half past 7
   c quarter to 5
4. a 9·20 or twenty past nine
   b 1·35 or twenty five to two
   c 11·55 or five to twelve
5. 4:40, quarter to five, 4:50,
   5 o'clock, 5:05, half past five

Ch 4 - Exercise 2 - *Page 42*

1. a half past four
   b quarter past five
   c quarter to two
   d half past eight
   e nine o'clock
   f quarter to seven
   g half past two
   h quarter to ten
   i quarter past eleven
   j half past nine
   k quarter past one
   l quarter to six
2. a 5:15   b 7:30   c 1:45
   d 11:15   e 7:45   f 10:30
3. a 9:30   b 1:15   c 8:45
   d 3:15   e 11:45   f 2:30
   g 7:15   h 10:45   i 6:30
4. a 5:10   b 11:40   c 3:53
   d 3:05   e 12:10   f 2:20
   g 6:45   h 11:30   i 6:40
   j 9:55   k 11:20   l 3:30

m 5:55   n 12:50   o 3:40
p 12:35   q 1:59   r 7:59

Ch 4 - Exercise 3 - *Page 45*

1. a eight o'clock in the morning
   or 8,00 am
   b half past eleven in the morning
   or 11·30 am
   c quarter past nine at night
   or 9:15 pm
   d half past 3 in the afternoon
   or 3:30 pm
   e twenty past six in the morning
   or 6·20 am
   f five past seven at night
   or 7·05 pm
   g 25 past 10 in the morning
   or 10·25 am
   h quarter to eight in the morning
   or 7·45 am
   i five to two in the morning
   or 1·55 am
   j ten to seven at night
   or 6·50 pm
   k five to eleven in the morning
   or 10·55 am
   l quarter past 1 in the afternoon
   or 1·15 pm
2. a 6·15 pm
   b 7·45 pm till 10·30 pm
   c 7·05 am till 7·50 am
   d 1·10 pm and 3·15 pm
   e 6·50 am and 7·55 am
   f 3·20 pm and 3·35 pm
3. a half past 2 in the afternoon
   b quarter to ten in the morning
   c ten to eleven at night
   d 8 mins to eight at night
   e ten past six in the morning
   f five to twelve in the morning
   g half past eleven in the morning
   h ten to seven at night
   i 25 to nine in the morning
   j 19 mins to 4 in the afternoon
   k 17 mins to six in the morning
   l 1 minute to 11 in the morning
   m 28 mins past 10 at night
   n 7 mins past 2 in the morning
   o 12 mins to 11 in the morning
   p 11 mins past 1 in the afternoon
   q 27 mins past 7 in the morning
   r 2 mins to 9 in the morning

Ch 4 - Exercise 4 - Page 48

1. a eight o'clock or 8:00
   b half past four or 4:30
   c quarter past 5 or 5:15
   d quarter to 11 or 10:45
   e ten to nine or 8:50
   f 25 past eleven or 11:25
2. Investigation

Ch 5 - Subtraction - Page 50

Ch 5 - Exercise 1 - Page 50

1. a 59   b 24   c 48   d 19
   e 48   f 75   g 88   h 74
   i 39   j 56   k 89   l 96
2. a 38   b 57   c 67   d 29
   e 45   f 25   g 88   h 67
3. 86 pages
4. 37 more girls
5. 68 people
6. 16 sums
7. 78 fewer
8. 7 large pieces

Ch 5 - Exercise 2 - Page 52

1. a 35   b 15   c 28   d 25
   e 70   f 48   g 27   h 58
   i 69   j 6   k 58   l 33
2. a 57   b 17   c 34   d 29
   e 14   f 28   g 29   h 29
   i 47   j 36   k 34   l 42
3. 48 balloons
4. 17 goals
5. 49 magazines
6. 18 more meetings
7. a 38p   b 19p
8. £52

Ch 5 - Exercise 3 - Page 54

1. a 121   b 242   c 180   d 203
   e 302   f 151   g 375   h 174
   i 532   j 347   k 500   l 76
2. a 111   b 751   c 1   d 163
   e 204   f 304   g 142   h 200
   i 312   j 21   k 351   l 315
   m 272   n 614   o 200   p 333

Ch 5 - Exercise 4 - Page 55

1. a 179   b 273   c 435   d 464
   e 469   f 79   g 144   h 336

   i 313   j 297   k 578   l 734
2. a 287   b 264   c 326   d 115
   e 198   f 66   g 84   h 48
   i 436   j 392   k 844   l 964
3. £188
4. £456
5. 315 ml
6. 482 tablets
7. 445 envelopes
8. 28 haystacks
9. 91 tadpoles
10. 290 people
11. £670
12. 91 miles
13. 272 units
14. 678 litres
15. £156
16. a £26   b £160   c £143   d £344
17. a £42   b £386
18. £324

Ch 5 - Exercise 5 - Page 59

1. a 77   b 116   c 46   d 612
   e 45   f 565   g 356   h 475
2. a 67   b 46   c 404   d 177
   e 461   f 481   g 364   h 647
3. 17 years
4. 28 bins
5. £118
6. £156

Ch 6 - Money - Page 61

Ch 6 - Exercise 1 - Page 61

1. a 10   b 20   c 20
2. a 50p, 20p, 5p
   b 50p, 20p, 20p, 5p, 2p, 2p
   c £1, 50p, 20p, 10p
3. a Daniel - 77p,
       Simon - £1 and 20p
   b £1 and 97p
   c (i) Simon   (ii) 43p
4. a £4 and 72p
   b £2 and 32p
   c £2 and 40p
5. a £5, £2
   b £10, £5, £1
   c £20, £5, £2, £1
   d £20, £20, £10, £5
   e £10, £1, 20p, 10p
   f £10, £5, £2, £2, 10p, 5p, 2p, 2p
   g £20, £10, £2, £1, 5p, 2p, 1p

   h £20, £20, £20, £5, £2,
      50p, 20p, 5p, 1p
6. 27p
7. £6 and 44p
8. a £6   b £11 and 50p
   c £70 and 1p

Ch 6 - Exercise 2 - Page 63

1. a £150 b £135
2. a £285 b Mr Johnson - £15 more
3. a £50, £50, £20, £5
   b £50, £50, £50, £20, £10, £5
   c 5 x £50, £10
   d 6 x £50 and 2 x £20
   e 9 x £50
   f 13 x £50 and £20 and £5
   g 16 x £50 and £10
   h 20 x £50
4. £165
5. a £170 b £227 c £107
   d £22 and 50p
6. a £15   b £35   c £25
   d £13 and 55p
7. No - should have £45 and 1p
   Only got £35 and 1p - £10 more
8. a Mr Smith - £125
     Mrs Smith - £85
     Mrs Alik - £215
     Mr Alik - £240
   b £365 c £300 c £65
9. a £115 b yes   c The Aliks
   d Microwave and Carpet
   e no   f £55
10. £137 and 50p
11. a milk, tie, shoes, laptop
    b various   c various
12. a-c various
13. a various
    b cheque, creditcard, debit card

Ch 7 - Measure 1 - Page 68

Ch 7 - Exercise 1 - Page 68

1. a A = 10 cm   B = 5 cm
     C = 2 cm   D = 13 cm
   b same
   c 2 cm, 5 cm, 10 cm, 13 cm
2. a 8 cm by 3 cm b 22 cm
3. a m   b cm   c mm
   d m   e mm   f cm
4. bus, ceiling, door, teacher,
   myself, desk

Year 3 Book   page 194   Answers

1. a 30 mm   b 22 mm
   c 51 mm   d 30 mm
2. a 28 mm   b 46 mm
   c 34 mm   d 30 mm
   e 20 mm   f 30 mm
   g 38 mm   h 8 mm
   i 9 mm
3. a 50 mm   b 70 mm
   c 100 mm   d 60 mm
   e 5 mm   f 95 mm
4. a 410 mm (± 2)   b 64 mm (± 2)
   c 73 mm (± 2)   d 79 mm (± 2)
   e 127 mm (± 2)   f 21 mm (± 2)
5. 50 mm, 46 mm, 69 mm (± 2)
6. a 65 mm, 79 mm, 28 mm, 29 mm
       (± 2 mm)   b 50 mm

Ch 7 - Exercise 3 - *Page 72*

1. a cm   b m   c mm   d cm
   e mm   f m   g m   h mm
2. a ruler   b ruler, measuring tape
   c metre stick, tape measure, ...
3. various
4. Sarah faster and probably
   more accurate
5. Investigations

Ch 7 - Exercise 4 - *Page 73*

1. 48 cm
2. a 30 cm b 43 cm c 274 m
3. 46 cm
4. a 20 cm   b 298 cm
   c 48 mm   d 500 cm
   e 136 mm   f 270 m
5. 20 cm
6. a 10 cm b 90 cm c 59 mm
7. a 10 cm b 5 cm

Ch 7 - Exercise 5 - *Page 75*

1. see drawings (allow ± 2 mm)
2. a see drawing (allow ± 2 mm)
   b/c 85 mm
3. See drawings (allow ± 2 mm)
4. a 42 cm   b 320 mm
   c 260 mm   d 260 mm
5. a see drawing (allow ± 2 mm)
   b 5 cm => Perimeter = 12 cm

Ch 8 - 2-D/3-D Shapes - *Page 77*

Ch 8 - Exercise 1 - *Page 77*

1. a triangle   b circle
   c rectangle   d square
   e hexagon   f half circle
2. a yes (3)   b yes (lots)
   c yes (2)   d yes (4)
   e yes (6)   f yes (1)
3. see drawings
4. a cube   b cylinder
   c triangle prism d squ pyramid
   e cuboid   f cone
5. a square
   b 2 circles and a rectangle
   c 2 triangles and 3 rectangles
   d 4 triangles and a square
   e 6 rectangles
   f 1 circle and 1 part circle

Ch 8 - Exercise 2 - *Page 78*

1. a yes   b no   c yes
   d no   e yes   f yes
2. various
3. a put 1 on top and 1 on bottom
   b both on top or bottom or ends
4. a yes   b no   c yes   d yes

Ch 8 - Exercise 3 - *Page 80*

1. a cuboid   b squ pyramid
   c triangle prism d squ pyramid
   e cylinder   f cone
2. a yes - cylinder
   b no
   c yes - square pyramid
   d no
3.

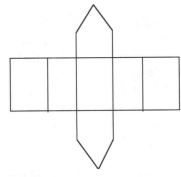

4. various

Ch 8 - Exercise 4 - *Page 82*

1. practical
2. practical
3. practical
4. a 192 cm
   b 140 cm
   c 155 cm
5. a practical   b 256 cm
6. Investigation

Ch 9 - Multiplication - *Page 85*

Ch 9 - Exercise 1 - *Page 85*

1. a 12   b 20   c 70   d 16
   e 35   f 50   g 18   h 40
   i 90   j 20   k 60   l 110
2. a 4   b 2   c 3   d 7
   e 6   f 4   g 12   h 11
   i 8   j 9   k 8   l 9
3. a 28   b 65   c 60   d 70
   e 75   f 56   g 80   h 86
   i 76   j 80   k 94   l 70
   m 95   n 100   o 120   p 85
4. 56 cans
5. 70 times
6. 70p
7. 90 sweets
8. 90 miles
9. 85 metres
10. 100p = £1

Ch 9 - Exercise 2 - *Page 88*

1. a 3   b 6   c 9
   d 12   e 15   f 18
   g 21   h 24   i 27
   j 30   k 33   l 36
2. Practical
3. a 3   b 6   c 7
   d 5   e 8   f 9
   g 10   h 0   i 12
4. a 15   b 21   c 33

Ch 9 - Exercise 3 - *Page 89*

1. a 42   b 75   c 93   d 126
   e 276   f 219   g 138   h 159
   i 171   j 267   k 147   l 195
2. a 51   b 39   c 78   d 90
   e 117   f 174   g 201   h 132
   i 162   j 240   k 288   l 216
3. a 75   b 210p c 141

4. a 156   b 168   c 155   d 225
   e 152   f 235   g 204   h 190
   i 194   j 282   k 480   l 154
5. 138 hours
6. 261
7. £234

Ch 9 - Exercise 4 - *Page 91*

1. a 16   b 20   c 12
   d 24   e 36   f 40
   g 28   h 32   i 48
2. a 5   b 2   c 4
   d 7   e 3   f 9
   g 11   h 0   i 8
3. a 56   b 108   c 172   d 136
   e 208   f 340   g 152   h 188
   i 280   j 388   k 356   l 304
4. a 112   b 212   c 184   d 116
   e 296   f 324   g 372   h 252
   i 140   j 52   k 272   l 360
5. a 180   b 76   c 148

Ch 9 - Exercise 5 - *Page 93*

1. a 32   b 16   c 48
   d 40   e 56   f 64
   g 80   h 72   i 96
2. a 6   b 3   c 0
   d 11   e 4   f 8
   g 7   h 9   i 10
3. 56 years old
4. 40 seconds
5. £32
6. 64 hours
7. 80 items
8. 48p
9. 72 lollies

Ch 9 - Exercise 6 - *Page 95*

1. a 136   b 256   c 312   d 360
   e 208   f 424   g 472   h 512
   i 568   j 624   k 664   l 680
   m 736   n 776   o 544   p 712
2. a 104   b 200   c 296   d 224
   e 352   f 416   g 464   h 320
   i 632   j 688   k 792   l 496
3. 240 sweets
4. £336
5. 600p (£6)
6. 704 sockets
7. 344 seats
8. 288 flags

9. 456 puffs

Ch 9 - Exercise 7 - *Page 97*

1. a 14   b 18   c 16   d 45
   e 56   f 18   g 24   h 28
   i 60   j 48   k 96   l 110
2. a 6   b 7   c 12   d 10
   e 9   f 8   g 6   h 11
   i 8   j 11   k 9   l 7
3. a 134   b 126   c 300   d 280
   e 435   f 544   g 370   h 176
   i 324   j 207   k 190   l 320
   m 275   n 584   o 800   p 231
4. 178p (£1 and 78p)
5. 225 bugs
6. £376
7. £320
8. £360
9. 232 pencils
10. 1000 apples

Ch 10 - Measure 1 - *Page 100*

Ch 10 - Exercise 1 - *Page 100*

1. bike - motor bike - mini -
   truck - bulldozer
2. pineapple
3. A (then B, then C)
4. a kg   b g   c g   d kg
5. sink
6. Watering can - Paint tin - Cola can
7. pot noodle
8. microwave - jug - cone -
   golf ball - eraser
9. a ml   b litres c litres d ml
10. 12 days

Ch 10 - Exercise 2 - *Page 102*

1. a 800 g   b 440 g
   c 813 g   d 3 kg 500 g
   e 4 kg 40 g   f 7 kg 660 g
2. a 700 g   b 291 g
   c 5 kg 800 g   d 1 kg 275 g
   e 9 kg 840 g   f 4 kg 227 g
3. a 610 g   b 895 g
   c 1 kg 910 g
4. 1 kg 50 g
5. a 1 kg 150 g   b 7 kg 650 g
6. 2 kg 10 g

Ch 10 - Exercise 3 - *Page 104*

1. a 800 ml
   b 510 ml
   c 794 ml
   d 3 litres 700 ml
   e 5 litres 40 ml
   f 10 litres 670 ml
2. a 900 ml
   b 270 ml
   c 5 litres 800 ml
   d 2 litres 925 ml
   e 8 litres 760 ml
   f 3 litres 475 ml
3. 250 ml ($\frac{1}{4}$ litre)
4. 290 litres 830 ml
5. 160 ml
6. 15 litres 835 ml
7. 6 litres 600 ml
8. 52 litres 830 ml

Ch 11 - Division 1 - *Page 107*

Ch 11 - Exercise 1 - *Page 107*

1. a 7   b 4   c 3   d 9
   e 9   f 8   g 9r1   h 9r2
   i 7 r 1 j 12r1 k 12r4   l 11r1
2. a 2   b 5   c 10   d 48
   e 100   f 100   g 2   h 5
   i 5   j 60   k 5   l 0
3. a 32   b 11   c 19   d 5
   e 16   f 38   g 19   h 3
   i 13r1 j 12r2 k 7   l 9r1
   m 36r1 n 16r3 o 9r6   p 3r2
4. 9 pieces
5. 33 chews
6. 38 packs
7. 12 trays
8. 35 ml
9. 30 full packs
10. a 14   b 2

Ch 11 - Exercise 2 - *Page 110*

1. a/b practical   c/d 4
2. a/b practical   c/d 5
3. a/b practical   c/d 6
4. a/b practical   c/d 7
5. a/b 8, 9, 10, 11, 12

Ch 11 - Exercise 3 - *Page 111*

1. a 3   b 2   c 5
      d 4   e 6   f 8
      g 7   h 9   i 10
2. a 21   b 9   c 18
      d 15   e 24   f 30
3. a 2   b 9   c 6
      d 4   e 10

Ch 11 - Exercise 4 - *Page 112*

1. a 13   b 22   c 10   d 23
      e 11   f 12   g 20   h 30
      i 21   j 31   k 32   l 33
2. 12 strawberries
3. 33 coins
4. 15 potatoes
5. 11 days

Ch 11 - Exercise 5 - *Page 114*

1. a 4r1   b 5r1   c 6r2   d 3r1
      e 2r1   f 4r2   g 6r1   h 8r2
      i 7r1   j 8r1   k 9r2   l 3r2
2. a 9   b 12   c 14   d 16
      e 17   f 19   g 24   h 26
      i 28   j 29   k 31   l 34
3. 18 cans
4. 27 books
5. 6 pieces
6. 24 parrots
7. a 10r2 b 11r1 c 20r1 d 11r2
      e 22r1 f 20r2 g 31r1 h 15r2
      i 24r1 j 27r2 k 29r1 l 30r2
8. a 5r2   b 22r2 c 16r1 d 24r2
9. a 14r1 b 17r2 c 6r2   d 3r1
      e 5r2   f 9r2   g 15r1 h 24r2
      i 25r1 j 28r1 k 32r2 l 34r1
10. 25 with 1 extra
11. 17 with 1 window over
12. 4 with 1 extra
13. 12
14. 28 with 2 extra
15. a 7   b 2

Ch 11 - Exercise 6 - *Page 117*

1. a 13r1 b 17   c 5r3   d 10r1
      e 22r1 f 12r2 g 20   h 15
      i 11r4 j 26   k 20r1 l 13r2
      m 22r1 n 6r9 o 27   p 38
2. 13 + 1 ml
3. 25 with 1 m left

4. 9 mins
5. a £39   b 33p

Ch 12 - Time 2 - *Page 119*

Ch 12 - Exercise 1 - *Page 119*

1. 60
2. a half past seven
   b quarter past two
   c quarter to four
   d five past eight
   e five to ten
   f three o'clock
3. a quarter past 9 in the morning
      or 9.15 am
   b 20 to 7 at night or 6.40 pm
   c 10 past 5 at night or 5.10 pm
   d 17 mins to 8 in the morning
      or 7.43 a2§m
   e quarter to 1 in the afternoon
      or 12.45 pm
   f 5 to 4 in the morning
      or 3.55 am
4. a 25 past 8 at night
   b quarter past 7 in the morning
   c 10 past 10 at night
   d 3 mins past 6 in the morning
   e 17 mins past 4 in the afternoon
   f 10 past 12 in the afternoon

Ch 12 - Exercise 2 - *Page 120*

1. a January   b December
   c Saturday   d Friday
   e October   f January
2. a 31   b 28(29) c 30   d 30
      e 31   f 31   g 30   h 31
3. a June   b March
   c October   d August
4. a 24/03/15   b 20/01/14
   c 23/06/11   d 19/09/18
   e 08/07/10   f 04/04/20
   g 11/12/09   h 02/02/17
   i 05/05/17
5. a 13th February 2012
   b 2nd April 2015
   c 10th October 2010
   d 22nd March 2004
   e 9th September 2009
   f 6th July 2016
   g 8th January 2020
   h 31st April 2015
   i 30th February 2010

6. There are only 30 days in April
   There are only 28 in Feb 2010
7. a 5   b Thursday
   c 24th Apr   d 31st March
8. a 9   b 3rd June
9. a Thursday 30th April
   b Thursday 2nd July 2015
   c Wednesday 1st July 2015
   d Friday 5th June 2015
   e Friday 22nd May 2015
   f Monday 1st June 2015
10. a 10   b 17   c 20
       d 2   e 12
11. a 10   b 5
12. Every 4 years from the last one.
    Various (2016, 2020, 2024, ...)

Ch 12 - Exercise 3 - *Page 123*

1. a min   b sec   c days   d hrs
      e secs   f hrs   g mins   h hrs
      i secs   j days
2. various
3. a 120   b 180   c 300   d 480
      e 30   f 240   g 600   h 1200
4. a 120   b 240   c 300   d 600
      e 180   g 30   h 60   h 15
5. Go through alphabet - 15 sec
   School Afternoon - two hours
   Walk a mile - 30 mins
6. Watch DVD - 2 hours
   Grow plant - five weeks
   Eat breakfast - ten mins
   Write name - eight secs
   Cycle round Yorkshire - 6 days
7. a Usain Bolt 9.58 secs 16/08/09
   b Hicham El Guerrouj
      3 min 43.13 secs in 1999
   c Wilson Kipsang 2 hrs 3.23 secs
      in 2013
   (These may need updated)
8. Practical

Ch 12 - Exercise 4 - *Page 125*

1. a-j - various
2. Practical
3. a 7 (tenths of a second)
   b various - track events
   c for accuracy

Ch 13 - Exercise 1 - Page 127

1. 4 times table
2. a 3   b 2   c 4
   d 6   e 5   f 7
   g 9   h 8   i 10
3. a 20   b 40   c 28
   d 24   e 36   f 32
4. a 8   b 10   c 7
   d 4   e 3   f £9
5. a 10   b 12   c 11
   d 20   e 21   f 22
6. a 21 sec b £12   c 22   d 10

Ch 13 - Exercise 2 - Page 130

1. a 3r1 b 2r3 c 3r2
   d 5r3 e 2r1 f 1r3
   g 4r2 h 3r3 i 4r3
2. a 10r2 b 10r3 c 11r2 d 12r1
   e 20r1 f 20r2 g 21r1 h 21r3
3. a 4r1 b 10r1 c 22r1
   d 3   e 63
4. a 7   b 8   c 10   d 13
   e 14   f 17   g 16   h 15
   i 18   j 19   k 23   l 24
5. a 9   b 12   c £21
   d 19   e £17
6. a 15r2 b 13r3 c 18r1 d 14r2
   e 17r3 f 23r1 g 18r2 h 23r3
   i 24r3 j 6r2 k 9r3 l 25r2
7. 15r3   b 17r2 c 16r1
   d 24r1 e 9r3 f 13 - 2 left
8. a 6r3 b 7r1 c 8r2 d 9r1
   e 11   f 12r3 g 14r1 h 15r1
   i 16r2 j 18   k 19r3 l 21r2

Ch 13 - Exercise 3 - Page 133

1. a 71r1 b 75   c 63   d 59r2
   e 58   f 67   g 57   h 97r1
   i 37r1 j 48r3 k 17r3 l 59r2
2. a 52r1 b 68r2 c 65r2
   d 60   e 29   f 30r1
   g 42r2 h 56r1 i 66r2
   j 70r1 k 47r4 l 75
   m 17   n 72r2 o 39r4
3. £86
4. 89 runs
5. 59 miles
6. £38

7. 82 bags - 1 left over
8. 65 ml
9. 35 boxes
10. 30

Ch 13 - Exercise 4 - Page 135

1. a 32   b 48   c 114 d 230
   e 235 f 165 g 9   h 13
   i 429 j 234 k 442 l 356
   m 392 n 34   o 218 p 666
   q 821 r 410 s 69   t 87r1
2. a 52   b 45   c 150 d 138
   e 55   f 120 g 291 h 14r1
   i 282 j 14   k 435 l 109
   m 581 n 923 o 840 p 26r2
   q 79   r 21   s 288 t 375
   u 240 v 28   w 10   x -1 (!!)
3. £141
4. 282 ladybirds
5. £123
6. 152 litres
7. 16 rows
8. 232 lollies
9. £483

Ch 14 - Statistics - Page 138

Ch 14 - Exercise 1 - Page 138

1. a 2.00   b Nursery
   c Decorating 3.15 - Paint Desk
2. a £100   b £290
   c £400 - in France
   d London - 3 nights
     or Cardiff - 1 week
3. a 20   b 45   c 40
4. a 4   b 8   c 20   d 16
   e 8   f 16   g girls

Ch 14 - Exercise 2 - Page 140

1. a 1   b 6   c 5
   d 4   e cinema f ice rink
   g 5   h 19   i 13
2. a 5   b 3   c 7
   d 0   e Duty f 19
3. a Bacon - 8   Cheese - 6
     Plain - 14   Vinegar - 4
     Pickle - 12
   b Plain   c Vinegar
   d 4   e 10   f 44
4. a 6   b 5
   c Freezer - 14 d 4

5. a 4's   b Cup Cake
   c 20   d 6
   e 12   f 30   g 6
6. a 100   b 170   c Holiday - 220
   d 40   e 570
7. a 4   b 22   c 7
   d 5   e 60

Ch 14 - Exercise 3 - Page 144

1. a |||| |||| b |||| |||| |||
   c |||| |||| |||| |||| ||||
   d |||| |||| |||| |||| |||| |||| |||| |

2.
   Masala   🍪🍪🍪🍪
   Madras   🍪🍪🍪🍪🍪
   Korma   🍪🍪🍪🍪
   Jalfrezi 🍪🍪🍪
   Balti   🍪🍪🍪

3. a

Word	Tally	Total
salt	||	2
fizzy	|||| |||| ||||		16
still	|||| ||	7
bottled	||||	5

   b 16   c 5   d 30
   e

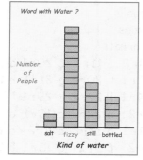
Word with Water ?
Number of People — salt, fizzy, still, bottled
Kind of water

Ch 14 - Exercise 4 - Page 145

1.

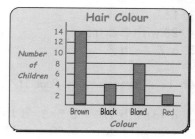
Hair Colour
Number of Children — Brown, Black, Blond, Red
Colour

2.

Favourite Drink

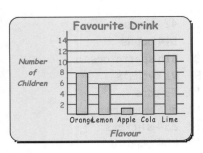

3.

Favourite Colours

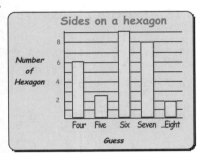

4.

Sides on a hexagon

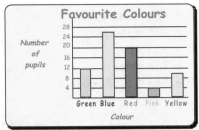

5.

Family Teddy Bears

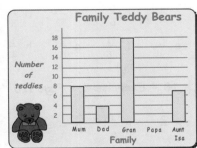

6.

Garden Creatures

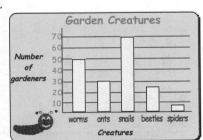

7.

Favourite Year Group

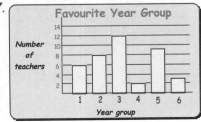

Ch 15 - Division 3 - *Page 149*

Ch 15 - Exercise 1 - *Page 149*

1. a 1   b 4   c 2
   d 7   e 3   f 5
2. a 64   b 16   c 32
   d 56   e 88   f 96
3. a 6   b 11   c 12   d 13
   e 17   f 30   g 36   h 18
   i 28   j 16   k 38   l 31
4. a 9   b 14   c 15
   d 19   e 37   f 50
5. a 6 seconds   b 4 sheep
   c 7 bikes   d 9 hams
   e 8 salesmen   f 5 days
   g 12 metres
6. 13 teams
7. £17 each
8. 25 vacuums
9. 14 hours
10. 33 weeks   11. £101
12. 21 per row
13. 27 paper clips

Ch 15 - Exercise 2 - *Page 152*

1. a 1r3   b 4r2   c 5r4
   d 6r4   e 6r7   f 7r6
   g 8r1   h 9r4   i 10r6
2. a 6r2   b 9r1   c 3r6   d 6r3
   e 10r5 f 8r7   g 10r1 h 9r3
   i 7r7   j 11r6 k 12r3 l 13r5
3. a 21r4 b 28r1 c 36r5 d 16r2
   e 18r6 f 37r4 g 15r7 h 18r3
4. a 6r3   b 8r5   c 13
   d 33r4 e 28r7 f 35r6
5. 11 with 2p left
6. 25 with 5 left
7. 28 with 6 left
8. 32 with 3 left
9. 36 tubs + 4 kg extra

Ch 15 - Exercise 3 - *Page 154*

1. a 37   b 19   c 16   d 13
   e 7   f 9r8   g 9   h 14r1
   i 57   j 86   k 33   l 99r1
   m 33r7 n 39r2 o 84   p 35r4
   q 58r4 r 96r2 s 28r3 t 41
2. a 24   b 34   c 19
   d 53r1 e 17r7 f 53
   g 28   h 79   i 63r1
   j 101   k 37   l 69

Ch 16 - Time 2 - *Page 157*

Ch 16 - Exercise 1 - *Page 157*

1. share it equally in two or ÷ 2
2. a 5p   b 9 g   c £14
   d 9 cm   e 20 m
3. 13 dolls
4. a/b

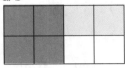

5. a $\frac{1}{2}$ b $\frac{3}{4}$ c $\frac{1}{3}$ d $\frac{1}{2}, \frac{2}{4}$
6. a $7\frac{1}{2}$ b $10\frac{3}{4}$

Ch 16 - Exercise 2 - *Page 158*

1. a $\frac{7}{10}$ b $2\frac{9}{10}$
2. a ..., $\frac{5}{10}$, $\frac{6}{10}$, ..., $\frac{8}{10}$
   b ..., $\frac{8}{10}$, ..., $\frac{6}{10}$, $\frac{5}{10}$, ...
3. see drawings
4. a $\frac{3}{10}$ b $\frac{5}{10}$ c $\frac{8}{10}$ d $\frac{9}{10}$
5. e $5\frac{2}{10}$ f $5\frac{3}{10}$ g $5\frac{5}{10}$
   h $5\frac{7}{10}$ i $5\frac{9}{10}$
6. j $7\frac{1}{10}$ k $7\frac{4}{10}$ l $7\frac{5}{10}$
   m $7\frac{6}{10}$ n $7\frac{9}{10}$ p $9\frac{2}{10}$
   q $9\frac{3}{10}$ r $9\frac{5}{10}$
   s $9\frac{8}{10}$ t $9\frac{9}{10}$
7. see drawings
8. See drawings
9. $\frac{7}{10}$

Ch 16 - Exercise 3 - *Page 161*

1. a $\frac{1}{3}$ b $\frac{1}{5}$ c $\frac{1}{6}$
   d $\frac{1}{9}$ e $\frac{1}{7}$ f $\frac{1}{17}$

2. a $1\frac{1}{4}$ b $5\frac{1}{3}$ c $6\frac{5}{6}$ d $3\frac{2}{5}$

   e $7\frac{2}{7}$ f $9\frac{5}{9}$ g $7\frac{3}{8}$ h $6\frac{5}{6}$

   i $4\frac{5}{7}$ j $9\frac{6}{17}$

3. See drawings
4. a half   b third
   c fifth   d eighth
5. a $\frac{1}{2}, \frac{1}{5}, \frac{1}{9}$

   b $\frac{1}{4}, \frac{1}{5}, \frac{1}{7}, \frac{1}{10}, \frac{1}{100}$

   c $\frac{1}{3}, \frac{1}{5}, \frac{1}{6}, \frac{1}{11}, \frac{1}{13}$

   d $\frac{1}{3}, \frac{1}{5}$, an eighth, a tenth

6. Practical
7. Investigation

Ch 16 - Exercise 4 - *Page 163*

1. $\frac{1}{6}$

2. a $\frac{1}{2}$ b $\frac{1}{3}$ c $\frac{1}{4}$ d $\frac{1}{5}$

   e $\frac{1}{6}$ f $\frac{1}{7}$ g $\frac{1}{8}$ h $\frac{1}{9}$

3. a $\frac{1}{3}$ b $\frac{1}{6}$ c $\frac{1}{8}$ d $\frac{1}{10}$

   e $\frac{1}{4}$ f $\frac{1}{9}$ g $\frac{1}{3}$ h $\frac{1}{8}$

   i $\frac{1}{6}$ j $\frac{1}{7}$ k $\frac{1}{5}$ l $\frac{1}{14}$

4. a 100   b $\frac{1}{100}$

5. $\frac{1}{6}$

Ch 16 - Exercise 5 - *Page 165*

1. a $\frac{1}{2}$ b $\frac{7}{8}$ c $\frac{2}{3}$ d $\frac{5}{7}$

   e $\frac{2}{3}$ f $\frac{8}{18}$ g $\frac{3}{4}$ h $\frac{13}{18}$

   i $\frac{3}{4}$ j $\frac{3}{5}$ k $\frac{5}{9}$ l $\frac{3}{4}$

2. a $\frac{1}{2}$ b $\frac{1}{8}$ c $\frac{1}{3}$ d $\frac{2}{7}$

   e $\frac{1}{3}$ f $\frac{10}{18}$ g $\frac{1}{4}$ h $\frac{5}{18}$

   i $\frac{1}{4}$ j $\frac{2}{5}$ k $\frac{4}{9}$ l $\frac{1}{4}$

3. a $\frac{4}{15}$ b $\frac{6}{15}$ c $\frac{1}{15}$ d $\frac{2}{15}$

4.

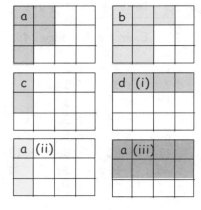

Ch 17 - 4 Operations - *Page 168*

Ch 17 - Exercise 1 - *Page 168*

1. a 20   b 7   c 79
   d 44   e 64   f 90
   g 47   h 37   i 60
2. a 73   b 47   c 38
   d 14   e 85   f 28r1
3. a 76   b 65   c (i) Jill (ii) 11
4. a 149p (£1 and 49p)
   b 109p b 84p

Ch 17 - Exercise 2 - *Page 169*

1. a 21   b 12   c 435
   d 16   e 40   f 107
   g 432   h 44   i 223
   j 911   k 96   l 9
   m 215   n 27   o 990
   p 403   q 51   r 276
   s 101   t 111   u 728
   v 20r3 w 80r2 x 26
2. a 945   b 603   c 94
   d 92   e 981   f 206
   g 102   h 43r1 i 330
   j 437   k 640   l 57r3
   m 783   n 24r1 o 216
   p 219   q 175   r 990
   s 59r2 t 308   u 17r5
   v 978   w 92   x 94
   y 257   z 900

Ch 17 - Exercise 3 - *Page 171*

1. 293 pupils
2. 219 boys
3. 248 times
4. 53 cars

5. £36 each
6. 42 chews
7. 144 pupils
8. 816 spectators
9. 91 cyclists
10. 73 cars
11. 696 workers
12. 234 stickers
13. 384 bananas
14. 840 piglets
15. a 428 passengers
    b 107 passengers
16. a 98 miles
    b 784 miles
17. a 342   b 171 guests

Ch 18 - Fractions 2 - *Page 175*

Ch 18 - Exercise 1 - *Page 175*

1. a $\frac{1}{6}$ b $\frac{1}{9}$ c $\frac{1}{7}$ d $\frac{1}{17}$

2. a $7\frac{2}{7}$ b $6\frac{5}{6}$

3. a $\frac{1}{5}$ b $\frac{1}{6}$ c $\frac{1}{10}$ d $\frac{1}{8}$

   e $\frac{2}{9}$ f $\frac{5}{16}$ g $\frac{3}{5}$ h $\frac{3}{4}$

4. a $\frac{4}{5}$ b $\frac{5}{6}$ c $\frac{9}{10}$ d $\frac{7}{8}$

   e $\frac{7}{9}$ f $\frac{11}{16}$ g $\frac{2}{5}$ h $\frac{1}{4}$

Ch 18 - Exercise 2 - *Page 176*

1. a $\frac{2}{3}$ b $\frac{4}{6}$ c $\frac{2}{3} = \frac{4}{6}$

2. $\frac{3}{4} = \frac{6}{8}$

3. a $\frac{2}{3} = \frac{4}{6}$ b $\frac{6}{10} = \frac{3}{5}$

   c $\frac{10}{12} = \frac{5}{6}$ d $\frac{2}{6} = \frac{1}{3}$

   e $\frac{10}{16} = \frac{5}{8}$ f $\frac{6}{9} = \frac{2}{3}$

4. a/c

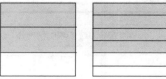

   b $\frac{2}{3}$ d $\frac{2}{3} = \frac{4}{6}$

Ch 18 - Exercise 3 - Page 178

1. a $\frac{1}{2}, \frac{1}{3}, \frac{1}{4}, \frac{1}{5}$ b $\frac{1}{5}, \frac{1}{4}, \frac{1}{3}, \frac{1}{2}$

2. a $\frac{1}{4} < \frac{1}{2}$ b $\frac{1}{5} < \frac{1}{3}$

   c $\frac{1}{2} > \frac{1}{5}$ d $\frac{1}{2} = \frac{2}{4}$

   e $\frac{1}{5} > \frac{1}{6}$ f $\frac{1}{3} < \frac{2}{3}$

   g $\frac{3}{4} > \frac{1}{4}$ h $\frac{1}{18} < \frac{1}{17}$

3. a $\frac{1}{2}, \frac{1}{4}, \frac{1}{5}, \frac{1}{8}$

   b $\frac{2}{4}, \frac{1}{3}, \frac{1}{4}, \frac{1}{5}, \frac{1}{6}, \frac{1}{10}$

   c half, third, quarter, fifth, sixth, ninth, fifteenth

Ch 18 - Exercise 4 - Page 179

1. a $\frac{2}{4}$ b $\frac{4}{5}$ c $\frac{4}{5}$ d $\frac{6}{8}$

   e $\frac{2}{4}$ f $\frac{2}{10}$ g $\frac{8}{16}$ h $\frac{1}{75}$

2. a $\frac{4}{4} = 1$ b $\frac{5}{5} = 1$ c $\frac{10}{10} = 1$

3. yes

4. $4\frac{2}{3}$

5. a $5\frac{2}{3}$ b $8\frac{2}{4}$ c $6\frac{2}{5}$

   d 1   e $5\frac{4}{7}$ f $3\frac{2}{4}$

Ch 19 - Revision - Page 181

1. a 230   b 685
2. a seventy eight
   b four hundred and nine
   c seven hundred and fifty three
   d nine hundred and ninety nine
3. a 150   b 630   c 370
4. a 7 units   b 8 tens
   c 3 hundreds
5. A is acute, B is obtuse, C is right
6. a 2   b 1   c 4
7. a green line   b brown line
8. vertical
9. obtuse angle
10. a 44   b 65   c 101   d 110
    e 843   f 792   g 861   h 913
11. 482 metres
12. December, November, October, September, August, July, June, May, April, March, February, January

13. III, IV, V, VI, VII, VIII, IX, X, XI, XII
14. a 9.20 or twenty past nine
    b 5.45 or quarter to six
    c 2.50 or ten to three
15. 6.30 am   b 9.45 pm
16. a 23   b 312   c 322   d 503
    e 44   f 458   g 279   h 295
17. a 53   b 419   c 169   d 149
18. a 743 stamps   b 165 stamps
19. a 25   b 100
20. a £4 and 80p
    b £20,£10,£5,£2,50p,20p,5p
    c No. It is £1 short
21. a 91 mm by 33 mm (± 2 mm)
    b 248 mm
22. a see drawing   b 75 mm
23. centimetres
24. a 4 triangles and a rectangle
    b 5 rectangles and 2 pentagons
      (5 sided shape)
25. 60 cm
26. A and C
27. a 111   b 164   c 330   d 348
    e 360   f 576   g 276   h 264
28. a 11   b 9   c 9   d 31
29. a 38   b 32   c 8r5   d 16
    e 34   f 43   g 35   h 86
30. a 19r1   b 59   c 62   d 39
    e 16   f 22   g 32   h 75
31. 30 boxes
32. a 9r4   b 69r1   c 50r1   d 87r1
    e 80r2   f 26r2   g 27r6   h 24r3
33. a Mon   b Thu   c January
34. a 31   b 366
35. a 3rd August 2014
    b 15/06/16
36. a ⵏⵏⵏ ⵏⵏⵏ III
    b ⵏⵏⵏ ⵏⵏⵏ ⵏⵏⵏ ⵏⵏⵏ ⵏⵏⵏ ⵏⵏⵏ IIII
37. a

Car	Tally	Total
Rolls-Royce	IIII	4
Ferrari	ⵏⵏⵏ IIII	9
Jaguar	ⵏⵏⵏ	5
Porsche	ⵏⵏⵏ I	6
Maserati	IIII	4
Lamborghini	II	2

   b 4   c 4

d

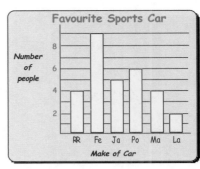

38. a

Drink	Tally	Total
cola	ⵏⵏⵏ II	7
fanta	IIII	4
lemonade	III	3
water	ⵏⵏⵏ	5
coffee	I	1

   b 7

   c

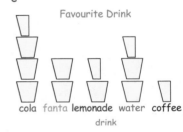

Favourite Drink

cola   fanta   lemonade   water   coffee
drink

39. a 7   b 14   c 118
40. a 5   b 14   c 33
41. a $\frac{3}{5}$ b $5\frac{7}{8}$
42. a $\frac{1}{6}$ b $\frac{4}{9}$ c $\frac{5}{8}$ d $\frac{9}{10}$
43. a $\frac{1}{2} = \frac{3}{6}$ b $\frac{1}{4} = \frac{2}{8}$

   c $\frac{2}{5} = \frac{4}{10}$

44. $\frac{1}{12}, \frac{1}{8}, \frac{1}{5}, \frac{1}{3}$

45. a $\frac{4}{5}$ b $\frac{2}{8}$ c 1   d $2\frac{4}{6}$
46. a 20   b 56   c 571
    d 344   e 256   f 323
    g 75   h 15   i 850
    j 49   k 212   l 90
47. a 180 kg   b 663 km
    c 36 people   d 270 g
48. a 680 g   b 140 ml
    c 7 kg 700 g
49. 1 kg 450 g